I WILL GO WITH THEE
AND BE THY GUIDE,
IN THY MOST NEED
TO GO BY THY SIDE

EVERYMAN'S LIBRARY
POCKET POETS

DONNE

······················

POEMS
AND
PROSE

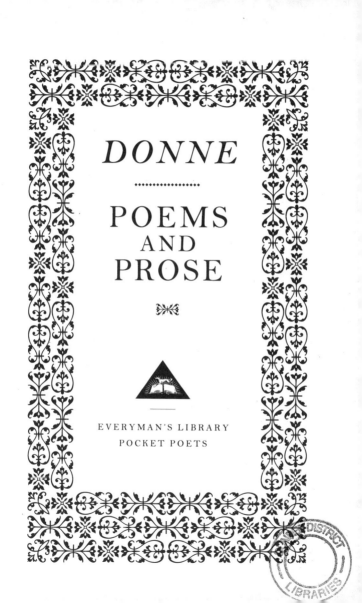

EVERYMAN'S LIBRARY
POCKET POETS

This selection by Peter Washington first published in
Everyman's Library, 1995
© David Campbell Publishers Ltd., 1995

ISBN 1-85715-722-2

A CIP catalogue record for this book is available from the British Library

Published by David Campbell Publishers Ltd.,
79 Berwick Street, London W1V 3PF

Distributed by Random House (UK) Ltd.,
20 Vauxhall Bridge Road, London SW1V 2SA

Typography by Peter B. Willberg

Typeset by Acc Computing, Queen Camel, Somerset

Printed and bound in Germany by
Mohndruck Graphische Betriebe GmbH, Gütersloh

CONTENTS

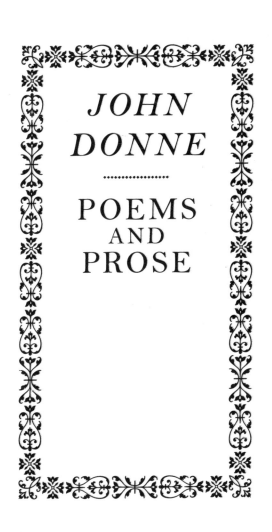

JOHN DONNE

POEMS
AND
PROSE

SONGS AND SONNETS

THE GOOD-MORROW

I wonder by my troth, what thou, and I
Did, till we lov'd? were we not wean'd till then?
But suck'd on countrey pleasures, childishly?
Or snorted we in the seaven sleepers den?
T'was so; But this, all pleasures fancies bee
If ever any beauty I did see,
Which I desir'd, and got, t'was but a dreame of thee.

And now good morrow to our waking soules,
Which watch not one another out of feare;
For love, all love of other sights controules,
And makes one little roome, an every where.
Let sea-discoverers to new worlds have gone,
Let Maps to other, worlds on worlds have showne,
Let us possesse one world, each hath one, and is one.

My face in thine eye, thine in mine appeares,
And true plaine hearts doe in the faces rest,
Where can we finde two better hemispheares
Without sharpe North, without declining West?
What ever dyes, was not mixt equally;
If our two loves be one, or, thou and I
Love so alike, that none doe slacken, none can die.

SONG

Goe, and catche a falling starre,
 Get with child a mandrake roote,
Tell me, where all past yeares are,
 Or who cleft the Divels foot,
Teach me to heare Mermaides singing,
Or to keep off envies stinging,
   And finde
   What winde
Serves to advance an honest minde.

If thou beest borne to strange sights,
 Things invisible to see,
Ride ten thousand daies and nights,
 Till age snow white haires on thee,
Thou, when thou retorn'st, wilt tell mee
All strange wonders that befell thee,
   And sweare
   No where
Lives a woman true, and faire.

If thou findst one, let mee know,
    Such a Pilgrimage were sweet,
Yet doe not, I would not goe,
    Though at next doore wee might meet,
Though shee were true, when you met her,
And last, till you write your letter,
                Yet shee
                Will bee
False, ere I come, to two, or three.

THE SUNNE RISING

     Busie old foole, unruly Sunne,
      Why dost thou thus,
Through windowes, and through curtaines call on us?
Must to thy motions lovers seasons run?
     Sawcy pedantique wretch, goe chide
     Late schoole boyes and sowre prentices,
  Goe tell Court-huntsmen, that the King will ride,
  Call countrey ants to harvest offices;
Love, all alike, no season knowes, nor clyme,
Nor houres, dayes, moneths, which are the rags of
     time.

     Thy beames, so reverend, and strong
      Why shouldst thou thinke?
I could eclipse and cloud them with a winke,
But that I would not lose her sight so long:
     If her eyes have not blinded thine,
     Looke, and to morrow late, tell mee,
  Whether both the'India's of spice and Myne
  Be where thou leftst them, or lie here with mee.
Aske for those Kings whom thou saw'st yesterday,
And thou shalt heare, All here in one bed lay.

She'is all States, and all Princes, I,
    Nothing else is.
Princes doe but play us, compar'd to this,
All honor's mimique; All wealth alchimie;
    Thou sunne art halfe as happy'as wee,
    In that the world's contracted thus.
  Thine age askes ease, and since thy duties bee
  To warme the world, that's done in warming us.
Shine here to us, and thou art every where;
This bed thy center is, these walls, thy spheare.

THE FLEA

Marke but this flea, and marke in this,
How little that which thou deny'st me is;
It suck'd me first, and now sucks thee,
And in this flea, our two bloods mingled bee;
Thou know'st that this cannot be said
A sinne, nor shame, nor loss of maidenhead,
   Yet this enjoyes before it wooe,
    And pamper'd swells with one blood made of two
    And this, alas, is more then wee would doe.

Oh stay, three lives in one flea spare,
Where wee almost, yea more then maryed are.
This flea is you and I, and this
Our mariage bed, and mariage temple is;
Though parents grudge, and you, w'are met,
And cloystered in these living walls of Jet.
   Though use make you apt to kill mee,
    Let not to that, selfe murder added bee,
    And sacrilege, three sinnes in killing three.

Cruell and sodaine, hast thou since
Purpled thy naile, in blood of innocence?
Wherein could this flea guilty bee,
Except in that drop which it suckt from thee?
Yet thou triumph'st, and saist that thou
Find'st not thy selfe, nor mee the weaker now;
    'Tis true, then learne how false, feares bee;
      Just so much honor, when thou yeeld'st to mee,
      Will wast, as this flea's death tooke life from thee.

THE CANONIZATION

For Godsake hold your tongue, and let me love,
   Or chide my palsie, or my gout,
My five gray haires, or ruin'd fortune flout,
    With wealth your state, your minde with Arts
      improve,
        Take you a course, get you a place,
        Observe his honour, or his grace,
Or the King's reall, or his stamped face
   Contemplate, what you will, approve,
   So you will let me love.

Alas, alas, who's injur'd by my love?
   What merchants ships have my sighs drown'd?
Who saies my teares have overflow'd his ground?
   When did my colds a forward spring remove?
      When did the heats which my veines fill
      Adde one more to the plaguie Bill?
Soldiers finde warres, and Lawyers finde out still
   Litigious men, which quarrels move,
   Though she and I do love.

Call us what you will, wee are made such by love;
   Call her one, mee another flye,
We'are Tapers too, and at our owne cost die,
   And wee in us finde the'Eagle and the dove,

The Phœnix ridle hath more wit
                By us, we two being one, are it.
So, to one neutrall thing both sexes fit,
                Wee dye and rise the same, and prove
                Mysterious by this love.

Wee can dye by it, if not live by love,
                And if unfit for tombes and hearse
Our legend bee, it will be fit for verse;
                And if no peece of Chronicle wee prove,
                        We'll build in sonnets pretty roomes;
                        As well a well wrought urne becomes
The greatest ashes, as half-acre tombes,
                And by these hymnes, all shall approve
                Us *Canoniz'd* for Love.

And thus invoke us; You whom reverend love
                Made one anothers hermitage;
You, to whom love was peace, that now is rage,
                Who did the whole worlds soule contract, and drove
                        Into the glasses of your eyes
                        So made such mirrors, and such spies,
That they did all to you epitomize,
                Countries, Townes, Courts: Beg from above
                A patterne of our love.

THE TRIPLE FOOLE

I am two fooles, I know,
For loving, and for saying so
    In whining Poëtry;
But where's that wiseman, that would not be I,
    If she would not deny?
Then as th'earths inward narrow crooked lanes
Do purge sea waters fretfull salt away,
    I thought, if I could draw my paines,
Through Rimes vexation, I should them allay,
Griefe brought to numbers cannot be so fierce,
For, he tames it, that fetters it in verse.

But when I have done so,
Some man, his art and voice to show,
    Doth Set and sing my paine,
And, by delighting many, frees againe
    Griefe, which verse did restraine.
To Love, and Griefe tribute of Verse belongs,
But not of such as pleases when'tis read,
    Both are increased by such songs:
For both their triumphs so are published,
And I, which was two fooles, do so grow three;
Who are a little wise, the best fooles bee.

WOMANS CONSTANCY

Now thou hast lov'd me one whole day,
To morrow when thou leav'st, what wilt thou say?
Wilt thou then Antedate some new made vow?
        Or say that now
We are not just those persons, which we were?
Or, that oathes made in reverentiall feare
Of Love, and his wrath, any may forsweare?
Or, as true deaths, true maryages untie,
So lovers contracts, images of those,
Binde but till sleep, deaths image, them unloose?
        Or, your owne end to Justifie,
For having purpos'd change, and falsehood; you
Can have no way but falsehood to be true?
Vaine lunatique, against these scapes I could
        Dispute, and conquer, if I would,
        Which I abstaine to doe,
For by to morrow, I may thinke so too.

SONG

Sweetest love, I do not goe,
   For wearinesse of thee,
Nor in hope the world can show
   A fitter Love for mee,
     But since that I
Must dye at last, 'tis best,
To use my selfe in jest
   Thus by fain'd deaths to dye;

Yesternight the Sunne went hence,
   And yet is here to day,
He hath no desire nor sense,
   Nor halfe so short a way:
     Then feare not mee,
But beleeve that I shall make
Speedier journeyes, since I take
   More wings and spurres than hee.

O how feeble is mans power,
   That if good fortune fall,
Cannot adde another houre,
   Nor a lost houre recall!

But come bad chance,
And wee joyne to'it our strength,
And wee teach it art and length,
  It selfe o'r us to'advance.

When thou sigh'st, thou sigh'st not winde,
  But sigh'st my soule away,
When thou weep'st, unkindly kinde,
  My lifes blood doth decay.
    It cannot bee
That thou lov'st mee, as thou say'st,
If in thine my life thou waste,
  Thou art the best of mee.

Let not thy divining heart
  Forethinke me any ill,
Destiny may take thy part,
  And may thy feares fulfill,
    But thinke that wee
Are but turn'd aside to sleepe;
They who one another keepe
  Alive, ne'r parted bee.

AIRE AND ANGELS

Twice or thrice had I loved thee,
Before I knew thy face or name;
So in a voice, so in a shapelesse flame,
Angells affect us oft, and worship'd bee,
    Still when, to where thou wert, I came
Some lovely glorious nothing I did see,
    But since, my soule, whose child love is,
Takes limmes of flesh, and else could nothing doe,
    More subtile than the parent is,
Love must not be, but take a body too,
    And therefore what thou wert, and who
        I did Love aske, and now
That it assume thy body, I allow,
And fixe it selfe in thy lip, eye, and brow.

Whilst thus to ballast love, I thought,
And so more steddily to have gone,
With wares which would sinke admiration,
I saw, I had loves pinnace overfraught,
    Ev'ry thy haire for love to worke upon
Is much too much, some fitter must be sought;
    For, nor in nothing, nor in things
Extreme, and scattring bright, can love inhere;
    Then as an Angell, face, and wings
Of aire, not pure as it, yet pure doth weare,
    So thy love may be my loves spheare;
        Just such disparitie
As is twixt Aire and Angells puritie,
T'wixt womens love, and mens will ever bee.

THE ANNIVERSARIE

    All Kings, and all their favorites,
    All glory of honors, beauties, wits,
The Sun it selfe, which makes times, as they passe,
Is elder by a yeare, now, then it was
When thou and I first one another saw:
All other things, to their destruction draw,
    Only our love hath no decay;
This, no to morrow hath, nor yesterday,
Running it never runs from us away,
But truly keepes his first, last, everlasting day.
    Two graves must hide thine and my coarse,
    If one might, death were no divorce,
Alas, as well as other Princes, wee,
(Who Prince enough in one another bee,)
Must leave at last in death, these eyes, and eares,
Oft fed with true oathes, and with sweet salt teares;
    But soules where nothing dwells but love
(All other thoughts being inmates) then shall prove
This, or a love increased there above,
When bodies to their graves, soules from their
      graves remove.

And then wee shall be throughly blest,
    But wee no more, then all the rest.
Here upon earth, we'are Kings, and none but wee
Can be such Kings, nor of such subjects bee;
Who is so safe as wee? where none can doe
Treason to us, except one of us two.
    True and false feares let us refraine,
Let us love nobly, and live, and adde againe
Yeares and yeares unto yeares, till we attaine
To write threescore, this is the second of our raigne.

TWICKNAM GARDEN

Blasted with sighs, and surrounded with teares,
    Hither I come to seeke the spring,
    And at mine eyes, and at mine eares,
Receive such balmes, as else cure every thing,
    But O, selfe traytor, I do bring
The spider love, which transubstantiates all,
    And can convert Manna to gall,
And that this place may thoroughly be thought
    True Paradise, I have the serpent brought.

'Twere wholsomer for mee, that winter did
    Benight the glory of this place,
    And that a grave frost did forbid
These trees to laugh and mocke mee to my face;
    But that I may not this disgrace
Indure, nor yet leave loving, Love let mee
    Some senslesse peece of this place bee;
Make me a mandrake, so I may grow here,
    Or a stone fountaine weeping out my yeare.

Hither with christall vyals, lovers come,
    And take my teares, which are loves wine,
    And try your mistresse Teares at home,
For all are false, that tast not just like mine;
    Alas, hearts do not in eyes shine,
Nor can you more judge womans thoughts by teares,
    Then by her shadow, what she weares.
O perverse sexe, where none is true but shee,
    Who's therefore true, because her truth kills mee.

THE DREAME

Deare love, for nothing lesse then thee
Would I have broke this happy dreame,
    It was a theame
For reason, much too strong for phantasie,
Therefore thou wakd'st me wisely; yet
My Dreame thou brok'st not, but continued'st it,
Thou art so truth, that thoughts of thee suffice,
To make dreames truths; and fables histories;
Enter these armes, for since thou thoughtst it best,
Not to dreame all my dreame, let's act the rest.

As lightning, or a Tapers light,
Thine eyes, and not thy noise wak'd mee;
    Yet I thought thee
(For thou lovest truth) an Angell, at first sight,
But when I saw thou sawest my heart,
And knew'st my thoughts, beyond an Angels art,
When thou knew'st what I dreamt, when thou
    knew'st when
Excess of joy would wake me, and cam'st then,
I must confesse, it could not chuse but bee
Prophane, to thinke thee any thing but thee.

Comming and staying show'd thee, thee,
But rising makes me doubt, that now,
      Thou art not thou.
That love is weake, where feare's as strong as hee;
'Tis not all spirit, pure, and brave,
If mixture it of *Feare, Shame, Honor,* have;
Perchance as torches which must ready bee,
Men light and put out, so thou deal'st with mee,
Thou cam'st to kindle, goest to come; Then I
Will dreame that hope againe, but else would die.

LOVES ALCHYMIE

Some that have deeper digg'd loves Myne then I,
Say, where his centrique happinesse doth lie:
      I have lov'd, and got, and told,
But should I love, get, tell, till I were old,
I should not finde that hidden mysterie;
      Oh, 'tis imposture all:
And as no chymique yet th'Elixar got,
      But glorifies his pregnant pot,
      If by the way to him befall
Some odoriferous thing, or medicinall,
    So, lovers dreame a rich and long delight,
    But get a winter-seeming summers night.

Our ease, our thrift, our honor, and our day,
Shall we, for this vaine Bubles shadow pay?
      Ends love in this, that my man,
Can be as happy'as I can; If he can
Endure the short scorne of a Bridegroomes play?
      That loving wretch that sweares,
'Tis not the bodies marry, but the mindes,
      Which he in her Angelique findes,
      Would sweare as justly, that he heares,
In that dayes rude hoarse minstralsey, the spheares.
      Hope not for minde in women; at their best,
      Sweetnesse, and wit they'are, but, *Mummy*, possest.

LOVES GROWTH

I scarce beleeve my love to be so pure
    As I had thought it was,
    Because it doth endure
Vicissitude, and season, as the grasse;
Me thinkes I lyed all winter, when I swore,
My love was infinite, if spring make'it more.
But if this medicine, love, which cures all sorrow
With more, not onely bee no quintessence,
But mixt of all stuffes, paining soule, or sense,
And of the Sunne his working vigour borrow,
Love's not so pure, and abstract, as they use
To say, which have no Mistresse but their Muse,
But as all else, being elemented too,
Love sometimes would contemplate, sometimes do.

And yet no greater, but more eminent,
    Love by the Spring is growne;
    As, in the firmament,
Starres by the Sunne are not inlarg'd, but showne,
Gentle love deeds, as blossomes on a bough,
From loves awakened root do bud out now.
If, as in water stir'd more circles bee
Produc'd by one, love such additions take,
Those like so many spheares, but one heaven make,
For, they are all concentrique unto thee,

35

And though each spring doe adde to love new heate,
As princes doe in times of action get
New taxes, and remit them not in peace,
No winter shall abate the springs encrease.

THE INDIFFERENT

I can love both faire and browne,
Her whom abundance melts, and her whom want
    betraies,
Her who loves lonenesse best, and her who maskes and
    plaies,
Her whom the country form'd, and whom the town,
Her who beleeves, and her who tries,
Her who still weepes with spungie eyes,
And her who is dry corke, and never cries;
I can love her, and her, and you and you,
I can love any, so she be not true.

Will no other vice content you?
Will it not serve your turn to do, as did your mothers?
Or have you all old vices spent, and now would finde
    out others?
Or doth a feare, that men are true, torment you?
Oh we are not, be not you so,
Let mee, and doe you, twenty know.
Rob mee, but binde me not, and let me goe.
Must I, who came to travaile thorow you,
Grow your fixt subject, because you are true?

Venus heard me sigh this song,
And by Loves sweetest Part, Variety, she swore,
She heard not this till now; and that it should be so
    no more.
She went, examin'd, and return'd ere long,
And said, alas, Some two or three
Poore Heretiques in love there bee,
Which thinke to stablish dangerous constancie.
But I have told them, since you will be true,
You shall be true to them, who'are false to you.

LOVES USURY

For every houre that thou wilt spare me now,
      I will allow,
Usurious God of Love, twenty to thee,
When with my browne, my gray haires equall bee;
Till then, Love, let my body raigne, and let
Mee travell, sojourne, snatch, plot, have, forget,
Resume my last yeares relict: thinke that yet
      We'had never met.

Let mee thinke any rivalls letter mine,
      And at next nine
Keepe midnights promise; mistake by the way
The maid, and tell the Lady of that delay;
Onely let mee love none, no, not the sport
From country grasse, to comfitures of Court,
Or cities quelque choses, let report
      My minde transport.

This bargaine's good; if when I'am old, I bee
      Inflam'd by thee,
If thine owne honour, or my shame, or paine,
Thou covet most, at that age thou shalt gaine.
Doe thy will then, then subject and degree,
And fruit of love, Love I submit to thee,
Spare mee till then, I'll beare it, though she bee
      One that loves mee.

LOVES DEITIE

I long to talke with some old lovers ghost,
    Who dyed before the god of Love was borne:
I cannot thinke that hee, who then lov'd most,
    Sunke so low, as to love one which did scorne.
But since this god produc'd a destinie,
And that vice-nature, custome, lets it be;
    I must love her, that loves not mee.

Sure, they which made him god, meant not so much:
    Nor he, in his young godhead practis'd it.
But when an even flame two hearts did touch,
    His office was indulgently to fit
Actives to passives. Correspondencie
Only his subject was; It cannot bee
    Love, till I love her, that loves mee.

But every moderne god will now extend
   His vast prerogative, as far as Jove.
To rage, to lust, to write to, to commend,
   All is the purlewe of the God of Love.
Oh were wee wak'ned by this Tyrannie
To ungod this child againe, it could not bee
   I should love her, who loves not mee.

Rebell and Atheist too, why murmure I,
   As though I felt the worst that love could doe?
Love may make me leave loving, or might trie
   A deeper plague, to make her love mee too,
Which since she loves before, I'am loth to see;
Falshood is worse than hate; and that must bee
   If shee whom I love, should love mee.

THE MESSAGE

Send home my long strayd eyes to mee,
Which (Oh) too long have dwelt on thee,
Yet since there they have learn'd such ill,
    Such forc'd fashions,
    And false passions,
      That they be
      Made by thee
Fit for no good sight, keep them still.

Send home my harmlesse heart againe,
Which no unworthy thought could staine,
Which if it be taught by thine
    To make jestings
    Of protestings,
      And breake both
      Word and oath,
Keepe it, for then 'tis none of mine.

Yet send me back my heart and eyes,
That I may know, and see thy lyes,
And may laugh and joy, when thou
    Art in anguish
    And dost languish
        For some one
        That will none,
Or prove as false as thou art now.

A NOCTURNALL UPON *S. LUCIES* DAY,
BEING THE SHORTEST DAY

Tis the yeares midnight, and it is the dayes,
Lucies, who scarce seaven houres herself unmaskes,
    The Sunne is spent, and now his flasks
    Send forth light squibs, no constant rayes;
        The worlds whole sap is sunke:
The generall balme th'hydroptique earth hath drunk,
Whither, as to the beds-feet life is shrunke,
Dead and enterr'd, yet all these seeme to laugh,
Compar'd with mee, who am their Epitaph.

Study me then, you who shall lovers bee
At the next world, that is, at the next Spring:
    For I am every dead thing,
    In whom love wrought new Alchimie.
        For his art did expresse
A quintessence even from nothingnesse,
From dull privations, and leane emptinesse
He ruin'd mee, and I am re-begot
Of absence, darknesse, death; things which are not.

All others, from all things, draw all that's good,
Life, soule, forme, spirit, whence they beeing have,
    I, by loves limbecke, am the grave
    Of all, that's nothing. Oft a flood

Have wee two wept, and so
Drownd the whole world, us two; oft did we grow
To be two Chaosses, when we did show
Care to ought else; and often absences
Withdrew our soules, and made us carcasses.

But I am by her death, (which word wrongs her)
Of the first nothing, the Elixer grown;
    Were I a man, that I were one,
    I needs must know, I should preferre,
        If I were any beast,
Some ends, some means; Yea plants, yea stones detest,
And love, all, all some properties invest,
If I an ordinary nothing were,
As shadow, a light, and body must be here.

But I am None; nor will my Sunne renew.
You lovers, for whose sake, the lesser Sunne
    At this time to the Goat is runne
    To fetch new lust, and give it you,
        Enjoy your summer all,
Since shee enjoyes her long nights festivall,
Let mee prepare towards her, and let mee call
This houre her Vigill, and her eve, since this
Both the yeares, and the dayes deep midnight is.

WITCHCRAFT BY A PICTURE

I fixe mine eye on thine, and there
    Pitty my picture burning in thine eye,
My picture drown'd in a transparent teare,
    When I looke lower I espie,
        Hadst thou the wicked skill
By pictures made and mard, to kill,
How many wayes mightst thou performe thy will?

But now I have drunke thy sweet salt teares,
    And though thou poure more I'll depart;
My picture vanish'd, vanish feares,
    That I can be endamag'd by that art;
        Though thou retaine of mee
One picture more, yet that will bee,
Being in thine owne heart, from all malice free.

THE BAITE

Come live with mee, and bee my love,
And wee will some new pleasures prove
Of golden sands, and christall brookes:
With silken lines, and silver hookes.

There will the river whispering runne
Warm'd by thy eyes, more than the Sunne.
And there the'inamor'd fish will stay,
Begging themselves they may betray.

When thou wilt swimme in that live bath,
Each fish, which every channell hath,
Will amorously to thee swimme,
Gladder to catch thee, than thou him.

If thou, to be so seene, beest loath,
By Sunne, or Moone, thou darknest both,
And if my selfe have leave to see,
I need not their light, having thee.

Let others freeze with angling reeds,
And cut their legges, with shells and weeds,
Or treacherously poore fish beset,
With strangling snare, or windowie net:

Let coarse bold hands, from slimy nest
The bedded fish in banks out-wrest,
Or curious traitors, sleavesilke flies
Bewitch poore fishes wandring eyes.

For thee, thou needst no such deceit,
For thou thy selfe art thine owne bait,
That fish, that is not catch'd thereby,
Alas, is wiser farre than I.

A VALEDICTION FORBIDDING MOURNING

As virtuous men passe mildly away,
   And whisper to their soules, to goe,
Whilst some of their sad friends doe say,
   The breath goes now, and some say, no.

So let us melt, and make no noise,
   No teare-floods, nor sigh-tempests move,
T'were prophanation of our joyes
   To tell the layetie our love.

Moving of th'earth brings harmes and feares,
   Men reckon what it did and meant,
But trepidation of the spheares,
   Though greater farre, is innocent.

Dull sublunary lovers love
   (Whose soule is sense) cannot admit
Absence, because it doth remove
   Those things which elemented it.

But we by a love, so much refin'd,
   That our selves know not what it is,
Inter-assured of the mind,
   Care lesse, eyes, lips, hands to misse.

Our two soules therefore, which are one,
　　　Though I must goe, endure not yet
A breach, but an expansion,
　　　Like gold to ayery thinnesse beate.

If they be two, they are two so
　　　As stiffe twin compasses are two,
Thy soule the fixt foot, makes no show
　　　To move, but doth, if the'other doe.

And though it in the center sit,
　　　Yet when the other far doth rome,
It leanes, and hearkens after it,
　　　And growes erect, as that comes home.

Such wilt thou be to mee, who must
　　　Like th'other foot, obliquely runne.
Thy firmnes makes my circle just,
　　　And makes me end, where I begunne.

A VALEDICTION OF WEEPING

      Let me powre forth
My teares before thy face, whil'st I stay here,
For thy face coines them, and thy stampe they beare,
And by this Mintage they are something worth,
      For thus they bee
      Pregnant of thee,
Fruits of much griefe they are, emblemes of more,
When a teare falls, that thou falst which it bore,
So thou and I are nothing then, when on a divers shore.

      On a round ball
A workeman that hath copies by, can lay
An Europe, Afrique, and an Asia,
And quickly make that, which was nothing, *All*,
      So doth each teare,
      Which thee doth weare,
A globe, yea world by that impression grow,
Till thy teares mixt with mine doe overflow
This world, by waters sent from thee, my heaven
      dissolved so.

O more then Moone,
Draw not up seas to drowne me in thy spheare,
Weepe me not dead, in thine armes, but forbeare
To teach the sea, what it may doe too soone,
     Let not the winde
     Example finde,
To doe me more harme, then it purposeth,
Since thou and I sigh one anothers breath,
Who e'r sighes most, is cruellest, and hastes the others
    death.

THE EXTASIE

Where, like a pillow on a bed,
    A Pregnant banke swel'd up, to rest
The violets reclining head,
    Sat we two, one anothers best;
Our hands were firmely cimented
    With a fast balme, which thence did spring,
Our eye-beames twisted, and did thred
    Our eyes, upon one double string,
So to'entergraft our hands, as yet
    Was all the meanes to make us one,
And pictures in our eyes to get
    Was all our propagation.
As 'twixt two equall Armies, Fate
    Suspends uncertaine victorie,
Our soules, (which to advance their state,
    Were gone out,) hung 'twixt her, and mee.
And whil'st our soules negotiate there,
    Wee like sepulchrall statues lay,
All day, the same our postures were,
    And wee said nothing, all the day.
If any, so by love refin'd,
    That he soules language understood,
And by good love were growen all minde,
    Within convenient distance stood,
He (though he knowes not which soul spake,

Because both meant, both spake the same)
Might thence a new concoction take,
    And part farre purer then he came.
This Extasie doth unperplex
    (We said) and tell us what we love,
Wee see by this, it was not sexe
    Wee see, we saw not what did move:
But as all severall soules containe
    Mixture of things, they know not what,
Love, these mixt soules, doth mixe againe,
    And makes both one, each this and that.
A single violet transplant,
    The strength, the colour, and the size,
(All which before was poore, and scant,)
    Redoubles still, and multiplies.
When love, with one another so
    Interinanimates two soules,
That abler soule, which thence doth flow,
    Defects of loneliness controules.
Wee then, who are this new soule, know,
    Of what we are compos'd, and made,
For, th'Atomies of which we grow,
    Are soules, whom no change can invade.
But O alas, so long, so farre
    Our bodies why doe wee forbeare?
They are ours, though not wee, Wee are
    The intelligences, they the spheares.

We owe them thankes, because they thus,
    Did us, to us, at first convay,
Yeelded their senses force to us,
    Nor are drosse to us, but allay.
On man heavens influence workes not so,
    But that it first imprints the ayre,
For soule into the soule may flow,
    Though it to body first repaire.
As our blood labours to beget
    Spirits, as like soules as it can,
Because such fingers need to knit
    That subtile knot, which makes us man:
So must pure lovers soules descend
    T'affections, and to faculties,
Which sense may reach and apprehend,
    Else a great Prince in prison lies.
To'our bodies turne wee then, that so
    Weake men on love reveal'd may looke;
Loves mysteries in soules doe grow,
    But yet the body is his booke.
And if some lover, such as wee,
    Have heard this dialogue of one,
Let him still marke us, he shall see
    Small change, when we'are to bodies gone.

THE WILL

Before I sigh my last gaspe, let me breath,
Great love, some Legacies; Here I bequeath
Mine eyes to *Argus*, if mine eyes can see,
If they be blinde, then Love, I give them thee;
My tongue to Fame; to'Embassadours mine
      eares;
    To women or the sea, my teares;
Thou, Love, hast taught mee heretofore
By making mee serve her who'had twenty more,
That I should give to none, but such, as had too much
      before.

My constancie I to the planets give,
My truth to them, who at the Court doe live;
Mine ingenuity and opennesse,
To Jesuites; to Buffones my pensivenesse;
My silence to'any, who abroad hath beene;
    My mony to a Capuchin.
Thou Love taught'st me, by appointing mee
To love there, where no love receiv'd can be,
Onely to give to such as have an incapacitie.

My faith I give to Roman Catholiques;
All my goods works unto the Schismaticks
Of Amsterdam: my best civility
And Courtship, to an Universitie;
My modesty I give to souldiers bare;
    My patience let gamesters share.
    Thou Love taughtst mee, by making mee
  Love her that holds my love disparity,
Onely to give to those that count my gifts indignity.

I give my reputation to those
Which were my friends; Mine industrie to foes;
To Schoolemen I bequeath my doubtfulnesse;
My sicknesse to Physitians, or excesse;
To Nature, all that I in Ryme have writ;
    And to my company my wit;
    Thou Love, by making mee adore
  Her, who begot this love in mee before,
Taughtst me to make, as though I gave, when I did but
       restore.

To him for whom the passing bell next tolls,
I give my physick bookes; my writen rowles
Of Morall counsels, I to Bedlam give;
My brazen medals, unto them which live
In want of bread; To them which passe among
    All forrainers, mine English tongue.
  Thou, Love, by making mee love one
Who thinkes her friendship a fit portion
For yonger lovers, dost my gifts thus disproportion.

    Therefore I'll give no more; But I'll undoe
The world by dying; because love dies too.
Then all your beauties will be no more worth
Then gold in Mines, where none doth draw it
      forth.
And all your graces no more use shall have
    Then a Sun dyall in a grave,
  Thou Love taughtst mee, by making mee
Love her, who doth neglect both mee and thee,
To'invent, and practise this one way, to'annihilate
    all three.

THE APPARITION

When by thy scorne, O murdresse, I am dead,
And that thou thinkst thee free
From all solicitation from mee,
Then shall my ghost come to thy bed,
And thee, fain'd vestall in worse armes shall see;
Then thy sicke taper will begin to winke,
And he, whose thou art then, being tyr'd before,
Will, if thou stirre, or pinch to wake him, thinke
  Thou call'st for more,
And in false sleepe will from thee shrinke,
And then poore Aspen wretch, neglected thou
Bath'd in a cold quicksilver sweat wilt lye
  A veryer ghost than I,
What I will say, I will not tell thee now,
Lest that preserve thee'; and since my love is spent,
I'had rather thou shouldst painfully repent,
Then by my threatnings rest still innocent.

A LECTURE UPON THE SHADOW

Stand still, and I will read to thee
A Lecture, Love, in loves philosophy.
    These three houres that we have spent,
    Walking here, Two shadowes went
Along with us, which we our selves produc'd;
But, now the Sunne is just above our head,
    We doe those shadowes tread;
    And to brave clearnesse all things are reduc'd.
  So whilst our infant loves did grow,
  Disguises did, and shadowes, flow,
  From us, and our cares; but, now 'tis not so.

That love hath not attain'd the high'st degree,
Which is still diligent lest others see.

Except our loves at this noone stay,
We shall new shadowes make the other way.
    As the first were made to blinde
    Others; these which come behinde
Will worke upon our selves, and blind our eyes.
If our loves faint, and westwardly decline;
    To me thou, falsly, thine,
    And I to thee mine actions shall disguise.
  The morning shadowes weare away,
  But these grow longer all the day,
  But oh, loves day is short, if love decay.

Love is a growing, or full constant light;
And his first minute, after noone, is night.

THE RELIQUE

When my grave is broke up againe
Some second guest to entertaine,
(For graves have learn'd that woman-head
To be to more then one a Bed)
And he that digs it, spies
A bracelet of bright haire about the bone,
Will he not let'us alone,
And thinke that there a loving couple lies,
Who thought that this device might be some way
To make their soules, at the last busie day,
Meet at this grave, and make a little stay?

If this fall in a time, or land,
Where mis-devotion doth command,
Then, he that digges us up, will bring
Us, to the Bishop, and the King,
To make us Reliques; then
Thou shalt be a Mary Magdalen, and I
A something else thereby;
All women shall adore us, and some men;
And since at such time, miracles are sought,
I would have that age by this paper taught
What miracles wee harmlesse lovers wrought.

First, we lov'd well and faithfully,
Yet knew not what wee lov'd, nor why,
Difference of sex no more wee knew,
Then our Guardian Angells doe,
    Comming and going, wee,
Perchance might kisse, but not between those meales.
    Our hands ne'r toucht the seales,
Which nature, injur'd by late law, sets free,
These miracles wee did; but now alas,
All measure, and all language, I should passe,
Should I tell what a miracle shee was.

THE LEGACIE

When I dyed last, and, Deare, I dye
  As often as from thee I goe,
  Though it be but an houre agoe,
And Lovers houres be full eternity,
I can remember yet, that I
  Something did say, and something did bestow;
Though I be dead, which sent mee, I should be
Mine owne executor and Legacie.

I heard mee say, Tell her anon,
  That my selfe, (that's you, not I,)
  Did kill me, and when I felt mee dye,
I bid mee send my heart, when I was gone,
But I alas could there finde none,
  When I had ripp'd me, 'and search'd where hearts
    did lye,
It kill'd mee againe, that I who still was true,
In life, in my last Will should cozen you.

Yet I found something like a heart,
     But colours it, and corners had,
     It was not good, it was not bad,
It was intire to none, and few had part.
As good as could be made by art
     It seem'd, and therefore for our losses sad,
I meant to send this heart in stead of mine,
But oh, no man could hold it, for twas thine.

THE DISSOLUTION

Shee'is dead; And all which die
   To their first Elements resolve;
And wee were mutuall Elements to us,
      And made of one another.
  My body then doth hers involve,
And those things whereof I consist, hereby
In me abundant grow, and burdenous,
      And nourish not, but smother.
  My fire of Passion, sighes of ayre,
Water of teares, and earthly sad despaire,
     Which my materialls bee,
But ne'r worne out by loves securitie,
Shee, to my losse, doth by her death repaire,
  And I might live long wretched so
But that my fire doth with my fuell grow.
     Now as those Active Kings
   Whose foraine conquest treasure brings,
Receive more, and spend more, and soonest breake:
This (which I am amaz'd that I can speake)
     This death, hath with my store
      My use encreas'd.
And so my soule more earnestly releas'd,
Will outstrip hers; As bullets flowen before
A latter bullet may o'rtake, the pouder being more.

66

THE PARADOX

No Lover saith, I love, nor any other
    Can judge a perfect Lover;
Hee thinkes that else none can or will agree,
    That any loves but hee:
I cannot say I lov'd, for who can say
    Hee was kill'd yesterday.
Love with excesse of heat, more yong then old,
    Death kills with too much cold;
Wee dye but once, and who lov'd last did die,
    Hee that saith twice, doth lye:
For though hee seeme to move, and stirre a while,
    It doth the sense beguile.
Such life is like the light which bideth yet
    When the lifes light is set,
Or like the heat, which fire in solid matter
    Leaves behinde, two houres after.
Once I lov'd and dyed; and am now become
    Mine Epitaph and Tombe.
Here dead men speake their last, and so do I;
    Love-slaine, loe, here I dye.

THE EXPIRATION

So, so, breake off this last lamenting kisse,
    Which sucks two soules, and vapors Both away,
Turne thou ghost that way, and let mee turne this,
    And let our selves benight our happiest day,
We aske none leave to love; nor will we owe
    Any, so cheape a death, as saying, Goe;

Goe; and if that word have not quite kil'd thee,
    Ease mee with death, by bidding mee goe too.
Oh, if it have, let my word worke on mee,
    And a just office on a murderer doe.
Except it be too late, to kill me so,
    Being double dead, going, and bidding, goe.

ELEGIES

ELEGIE XVI
On his Mistris

By our first strange and fatall interview,
By all desires which thereof did ensue,
By our long starving hopes, by that remorse
Which my words masculine perswasive force
Begot in thee, and by the memory
Of hurts, which spies and rivals threatned me,
I calmly beg. But by thy fathers wrath,
By all paines, which want and divorcement hath,
I conjure thee, and all the oathes which I
And thou have sworne to seale joynt constancy,
Here I unsweare, and overswear them thus,
Thou shalt not love by wayes so dangerous.
Temper, ô faire Love, loves impetuous rage,
Be my true Mistris still, not my faign'd Page;
I'll goe, and, by thy kinde leave, leave behinde
Thee, onely worthy to nurse in my minde,
Thirst to come backe; ô if thou die before,
My soule from other lands to thee shall soare.
Thy (else Almighty) beautie cannot move
Rage from the Seas, nor thy love teach them love,
Nor tame wilde Boreas harshnesse; Thou has reade
How roughly hee in pecces shivered
Faire Orithea, whom he swore he lov'd.
Fall ill or good, 'tis madnesse to have prov'd

Dangers unurg'd; Feed on this flattery,
That absent Lovers one in th'other be.
Dissemble nothing, not a boy, nor change
Thy bodies habite, nor mindes; bee not strange
To thy selfe onely. All will spie in thy face
A blushing womanly discovering grace;
Richly cloath'd Apes, are call'd Apes, and as soone
Ecclips'd as bright we call the Moone the Moone.
Men of France, changeable Camelions,
Spittles of diseases, shops of fashions,
Loves fuellers, and the rightest company
Of Players, which upon the worlds stage be,
Will quickly know thee, and no lesse, alas!
Th'indifferent Italian, as we passe
His warme land, well content to thinke thee Page,
Will hunt thee with such lust, and hideous rage,
As *Lots* faire guests were vext. But none of these
Nor spungy hydroptique Dutch shall thee displease,
If thou stay here. O stay here, for, for thee
England is onely a worthy Gallerie,
To walke in expectation, till from thence
Our greatest King call thee to his presence.
When I am gone, dreame me some happinesse,
Nor let thy lookes our long hid love confesse,
Nor praise, nor dispraise me, nor blesse nor curse
Openly loves force, nor in bed fright thy Nurse
With midnights startings, crying out, oh, oh

Nurse, ô my love is slaine, I saw him goe
O'r the white Alpes alone; I saw him I,
Assail'd, fight, taken, stabb'd, bleed, fall, and die.
Augure me better chance, except dread *Jove*
Thinke it enough for me to'have had thy love.

ELEGIE XIX
To his Mistress Going to Bed

Come, Madam, come, all rest my powers defie,
Until I labour, I in labour lie.
The foe oft-times having the foe in sight,
Is tir'd with standing though he never fight.
Off with that girdle, like heavens Zone glittering,
But a far fairer world incompassing.
Unpin that spangled breastplate which you wear,
That th'eyes of busie fooles may be stopt there.
Unlace your self, for that harmonious chyme,
Tells me from you, that now it is bed time.
Off with that happy busk, which I envie,
That still can be, and still can stand so nigh.
Your gown going off, such beautious state reveals,
As when from flowry meads th'hills shadowe steales.
Off with that wyerie Coronet and shew
The haiery Diademe which on you doth grow:
Now off with those shooes, and then softly tread
In this loves hallow'd temple, this soft bed.
In such white robes, heaven's Angels us'd to be
Receavd by men: thou Angel bringst with thee
A heaven like Mahomets Paradice, and though
Ill spirits walk in white, we easly know,
By this these Angels from an evil sprite,
Those set our hairs, but these our flesh upright.

Licence my roaving hands, and let them go,
Before, behind, between, above, below.
O my America! my new-found-land,
My kingdome, safeliest when with one man man'd,
My Myne of precious stones: My Emperie,
How blest am I in this discovering thee!
To enter in these bonds, is to be free;
Then where my hand is set, my seal shall be.
   Full nakedness! All joyes are due to thee,
As souls unbodied, bodies uncloth'd must be,
To taste whole joyes. Jems which you women use
Are like Atlanta's balls, cast in mens views,
That when a fools eye lighteth on a Jem,
His earthly soul may covet theirs, not them:
Like pictures, or like books gay coverings made
For lay-men, are all women thus array'd.
Themselves are mystick books, which only wee
(Whom their imputed grace will dignifie)
Must see reveal'd. Then since that I may know;
As liberally, as to a Midwife shew
Thy self: cast all, yea, this white lynnen hence,
There is no pennance, much less innocence:
   To teach thee, I am naked first; why then
What needst thou have more covering then a man.

ELEGIE XVII

The heavens rejoyce in motion, why should I
Abjure my so much lov'd variety,
And not with many youth and love divide?
Pleasure is none, if not diversifi'd:
The sun that sitting in the chaire of light
Sheds flame into what else soever doth seem bright,
Is not contented at one Signe to Inne,
But ends his year and with a new beginnes.
All things doe willingly in change delight,
The fruitfull mother of our appetite:
Rivers the clearer and more pleasing are,
Where their fair spreading streames run wide and farr;
And a dead lake that no strange bark doth greet,
Corrupts it self and what doth live in it.
Let no man tell me such a one is faire,
And worthy all alone my love to share.
Nature in her hath done the liberall part
Of a kinde Mistresse, and imploy'd her art
To make her loveable, and I aver
Him not humane that would turn back from her:
I love her well, and would, if need were, dye
To doe her service. But followes it that I
Must serve her onely, when I may have choice?
The law is hard, and shall not have my voice.
The last I saw in all extreames is faire,

And holds me in the Sun-beames of her haire;
Her nymph-like features such agreements have
That I could venture with her to the grave:
Another's brown, I like her not the worse,
Her tongue is soft and takes me with discourse:
Others, for that they well descended are,
Do in my love obtain as large a share;
And though they be not fair, 'tis much with mee
To win their love onely for their degree.
And though I faile of my required ends,
The attempt is glorious and it selfe commends.
How happy were our Syres in ancient times
Who held plurality of loves no crime!
With them it was accounted charity
To stirre up race of all indifferently;
Kindreds were not exempted from the bands:
Which with the Persian still in usage stands.
Women were then no sooner asked then won,
And what they did was honest and well done.
But since this title honour hath been us'd,
Our weake credulity hath been abus'd;
The golden laws of nature are repeald,
Which our first Fathers in such reverence held;
Our liberty revers'd and Charter's gone,
And we made servants to opinion,
A monster in no certain shape attir'd,
And whose originall is much desir'd,

Formlesse at first, but growing on it fashions,
And doth prescribe manners and laws to nations.
Here love receiv'd immedicable harmes,
And was dispoiled of his daring armes.
A greater want then is his daring eyes,
He lost those awfull wings with which he flies;
His sinewy bow, and those immortall darts
Wherewith he'is wont to bruise resisting hearts;
Onely some few strong in themselves and free
Retain the seeds of antient liberty,
Following that part of love although deprest,
And make a throne for him within their brest,
In spight of modern censures him avowing
Their Soveraigne, all service him allowing.
Amongst which troop although I am the least,
Yet equall in perfection with the best,
I glory in subjection of his hand,
Nor ever did decline his least command:
For in whatever forme the message came
My heart did open and receive the same.
But time will in his course a point discry
When I this loved service must deny.
For our allegiance temporary is,
With firmer age returnes our liberties.
What time in years and judgement we repos'd,
Shall not so easily be to change dispos'd
Nor to the art of severall eyes obeying,

But beauty with true worth securely weighing,
Which being found assembled in some one
Wee'l leave her ever, and love her alone.

SATIRES

SATYRE I

Away thou fondling motley humorist,
Leave mee, and in this standing woodden chest,
Consorted with these few bookes, let me lye
In prison, and here be coffin'd, when I dye;
Here are Gods conduits, grave Divines; and here
Natures Secretary, the Philosopher;
And jolly Statesmen, which teach how to tie
The sinewes of a cities mistique bodie;
Here gathering Chroniclers, and by them stand
Giddie fantastique Poëts of each land.
Shall I leave all this constant company,
And follow headlong, wild uncertaine thee?
First sweare by thy best love in earnest
(If thou which lov'st all, canst love any best)
Thou wilt not leave mee in the middle street,
Though some more spruce companion thou dost meet
Not though a Captaine do come in thy way
Bright parcell gilt, with forty dead mens pay,
Not though a briske perfum'd piert Courtier
Deigne with a nod, thy courtesie to answer.
Nor come a velvet Justice with a long
Great traine of blew coats, twelve, or fourteen strong,
Wilt thou grin or fawne on him, or prepare
A speech to Court his beautious sonne and heire!
For better or worse take mee, or leave mee:

To take, and leave mee is adultery.
Oh monstrous, superstitious puritan,
Of refin'd manners, yet ceremoniall man,
That when thou meet'st one, with enquiring eyes
Dost search, and like a needy broker prize
The silke, and gold he weares, and to that rate
So high or low, dost raise thy formall hat:
That wilt consort none, untill thou have knowne
What lands hee hath in hope, or of his owne,
As though all thy companions should make thee
Jointures, and marry thy deare company.
Why should'st thou that dost not onely approve,
But in ranke itchie lust, desire, and love
The nakednesse and barenesse to enjoy,
Of thy plumpe muddy whore, or prostitute boy
Hate vertue, though shee be naked, and bare?
At birth, and death, our bodies naked are;
And till our Soules be unapparrelled
Of bodies, they from blisse are banished.
Mans first blest state was naked, when by sinne
Hee lost that, yet hee was cloath'd but in beasts skin,
And in this course attire, which I now weare,
With God, and with the Muses I conferre.
But since thou like a contrite penitent,
Charitably warn'd of thy sinnes, dost repent
These vanities, and giddinesse, loe
I shut my chamber doore, and come, lets goe.

But sooner may a cheape whore, who hath beene
Worne by as many severall men in sinne,
As are black feathers, or musk-colour hose,
Name her childs right true father, 'mongst all those:
Sooner may one guesse, who shall beare away
The infant of London, Heire to an India,
And sooner may a gulling weather-Spie
By drawing forth heavens Scheme tell certainly
What fashioned hats, or ruffes, or suits next yeare
Our subtile-witted antique youths will weare;
Then thou, when thou depart'st from mee, canst show
Whither, why, when, or with whom thou wouldst go.
But how shall I be pardon'd my offence
That thus have sinn'd against my conscience?
Now we are in the street; He first of all
Improvidently proud, creepes to the wall,
And so imprisoned, and hem'd in by mee
Sells for a little state his libertie,
Yet though he cannot skip forth now to greet
Every fine silken painted foole we meet,
He them to him with amorous smiles allures,
And grins, smacks, shrugs, and such an itch endures,
As prentises, or schoole-boyes which doe know
Of some gay sport abroad, yet dare not goe.
And as fidlers stop lowest, at highest sound,
So to the most brave, stoops hee nigh'st the ground.
But to a grave man, he doth move no more

Then the wise politique horse would heretofore,
Or thou O Elephant or Ape wilt doe,
When any names the King of Spaine to you.
Now leaps he upright, Joggs me, and cryes, Do you see
Yonder well favoured youth? Which? Oh, 'tis hee
That dances so divinely; Oh, said I,
Stand still, must you dance here for company?
Hee droopt, wee went, till one (which did excell
Th'Indians, in drinking his Tobacco well)
Met us; they talk'd; I whispered, let'us goe,
'T may be you smell him not, truely I doe;
He heares not mee, but, on the other side
A many-coloured Peacock having spide,
Leaves him and mee; I for my lost sheep stay;
He followes, overtakes, goes on the way,
Saying, him whom I last left, all repute
For his device, in hansoming a sute,
To judge of lace, pinke, panes, print, cut, and plight,
Of all the Court, to have the best conceit;
Our dull Comedians want him, let him goe;
But Oh, God strengthen thee, why stoop'st thou so?
Why, he hath travayld. Long? No, but to me
Which understand none, he doth seeme to be
Perfect French, and Italian; I replyed,
So is the Poxe; He answered not, but spy'd
More men of sort, of parts, and qualities;
At last his Love he in a windowe spies,

And like light dew exhal'd, he flings from mee
Violently ravish'd to his lechery.
Many were there, he could command no more;
Hee quarrell'd, fought, bled; and turn'd out of dore
    Directly came to mee hanging the head,
     And constantly a while must keepe his bed.

SATYRE II

Sir; though (I thanke God for it) I do hate
Perfectly all this towne, yet there's one state
In all ill things so excellently best,
That hate, toward them, breeds pitty towards the rest.
Though Poëtry indeed be such a sinne
As I thinke that brings dearths, and Spaniards in,
Though like the Pestilence and old fashion'd love,
Ridlingly it catch men; and doth remove
Never, till it be sterv'd out; yet their state
Is poore, disarm'd, like Papists, not worth hate.
One, (like a wretch, which at Barre judg'd as dead,
Yet prompts him which stands next, and cannot reade,
And saves his life) gives ideot actors meanes
(Starving himselfe) to live by his labor'd sceanes;
As in some Organ, Puppits dance above
And bellows pant below, which them do move.
One would move Love by rithmes; but witchcrafts
          charms
Bring not now their old feares, nor their old harmes:
Rammes, and slings now are seely battery,
Pistolets are the best Artillerie.
And they who write to Lords, rewards to get,
Are they not like singers at doores for meat?
And they who write, because all write, have still
That excuse for writing, and for writing ill;

But hee is worst, who (beggarly) doth chaw
Others wits fruits, and in his ravenous maw
Rankly digested, doth those things out-spue,
As his owne things; and they are his owne, 'tis true,
For if one eate my meate, though it be knowne
The meate was mine, th'excrement is his owne:
But these do mee no harme, nor they which use
To out-doe Dildoes, and out-usure Jewes;
To out-drinke the sea, to out-sweare the Letanie;
Who with sinnes all kindes as familiar bee
As Confessors; and for whose sinfull sake,
Schoolemen new tenements in hell must make:
Whose strange sinnes, Canonists could hardly tell
In which Commandements large receit they dwell.
But these punish themselves; the insolence
Of Coscus onely breeds my just offence,
Whom time (which rots all, and makes botches poxe,
And plodding on, must make a calfe an oxe)
Hath made a Lawyer, which was (alas) of late
But a scarce Poët; jollier of this state,
Then are new benefic'd ministers, he throwes
Like nets, or lime-twigs, wheresoever he goes,
His title of Barrister, on every wench,
And wooes in language of the Pleas, and Bench:
A motion, Lady; Speake Coscus; I have beene
In love, ever since *tricesimo* of the Queene,
Continuall claimes I have made, injunctions got

To stay my rivals suit, that hee should not
Proceed, spare mee; In Hillary terme I went,
You said, If I return'd next size in Lent,
I should be in remitter of your grace;
In th'interim my letters should take place
Of affidavits: words, words, which would teare
The tender labyrinth of a soft maids eare,
More, more, then ten Sclavonians scolding, more
Then when winds in our ruin'd Abbeyes rore;
Which sicke with Poëtrie, and possest with muse
Thou wast, and mad, I hop'd; but men which chuse
Law practise for meere gaine, bold soule, repute
Worse then imbrothel'd strumpets prostitute.
Now like an owlelike watchman, hee must walke
His hand still at a bill, now he must talke
Idly, like prisoners, which whole months will sweare
That onely suretiship hath brought them there,
And to every suitor lye in every thing,
Like a Kings favourite, yea like a King;
Like a wedge in a blocke, wring to the barre,
Bearing like Asses, and more shamelesse farre
Then carted whores, lye, to the grave Judge; for
Bastardy abounds not in Kings titles, nor
Symonie and Sodomy in Churchmens lives,
As these things do in him; by these he thrives.
Shortly (as the sea) hee will compasse all the land,
From Scots, to Wight; from Mount, to Dover strand.

And spying heires melting with luxurie,
Satan will not joy at their sinnes, as hee.
For as a thrifty wench scrapes kitching-stuffe,
And barrelling the droppings, and the snuffe,
Of wasting candles, which in thirty yeare
(Relique-like kept) perchance buyes wedding geare;
Peecemeale he gets lands, and spends as much time
Wringing each Acre, as men pulling prime.
In parchment then, large as his fields, hee drawes
Assurances, bigge, as gloss'd civill lawes,
So huge, that men (in our times forwardnesse)
Are Fathers of the Church for writing lesse.
These hee writes not; nor for these written payes,
Therefore spares no length; as in those first dayes
When Luther was profest, He did desire
Short *Pater nosters*, saying as a Fryer
Each day his beads, but having left those lawes,
Addes to Christs prayer, the Power and glory clause.
But when he sells or changes land, he'impaires
His writings, and (unwatch'd) leaves out, *ses heires*,
As slily as any Commentator goes by
Hard words, or sense; or in Divinity
As controverters, in vouch'd Texts, leave out
Shrewd words, which might against them cleare the
    doubt.
Where are those spred woods which cloth'd hertofore
Those bought lands? not built, nor burnt within dore.

Where's th'old landlords troops, and almes? In great hals
Carthusian fasts, and fulsome Bachanalls
Equally I hate; meanes blesse; in rich mens homes
I bid kill some beasts, but no Hecatombs,
None starve, none surfet so; But (Oh) we allow,
Good workes as good, but out of fashion now,
Like old rich wardrops; but my words none drawes
Within the vast reach of th'huge statute lawes.

SATYRE III

Kinde pitty chokes my spleene; brave scorn forbids
Those teares to issue which swell my eye-lids;
I must not laugh, nor weepe sinnes, and be wise,
Can railing then cure these worne maladies?
Is not our Mistresse faire Religion,
As worthy of all our Soules devotion,
As vertue was to the first blinded age?
Are not heavens joyes as valiant to asswage
Lusts, as earths honour was to them? Alas,
As wee do them in meanes, shall they surpasse
Us in the end, and shall thy fathers spirit
Meete blinde Philosophers in heaven, whose merit
Of strict life may be imputed faith, and heare
Thee, whom hee taught so easie wayes and neare
To follow, damn'd? O if thou dar'st, feare this.
This feare great courage, and high valour is;
Dar'st thou ayd mutinous Dutch, and dar'st thou lay
Thee in ships wooddden Sepulchers, a prey
To leaders rage, to stormes, to shot, to dearth?
Dar'st thou dive seas, and dungeons of the earth?
Hast thou couragious fire to thaw the ice
Of frozen North discoveries? and thrise
Colder then Salamanders, like divine
Children in th'oven, fires of Spaine, and the line,
Whose countries limbecks to our bodies bee,

Canst thou for gaine beare? and must every hee
Which cryes not, Goddesse, to thy Mistresse, draw,
Or eat thy poysonous words? courage of straw!
O desperate coward, wilt thou seeme bold, and
To thy foes and his (who made thee to stand
Sentinell in his worlds garrison) thus yeeld,
And for the forbidden warres, leave th'appointed field?
Know thy foe, the foule devill h'is, whom thou
Strivest to please: for hate, not love, would allow
Thee faine, his whole Realme to be quit; and as
The worlds all parts wither away and passe,
So the worlds selfe, thy other lov'd foe, is
In her decrepit wayne, and thou loving this,
Dost love a withered and worne strumpet; last,
Flesh (it selfes death) and joyes which flesh can taste,
Thou lovest; and thy faire goodly soule, which doth
Give this flesh power to taste joy, thou dost loath;
Seeke true religion. O where? Mirreus
Thinking her unhous'd here, and fled from us,
Seekes her at Rome, there, because hee doth know
That shee was there a thousand yeares agoe,
He loves her ragges so, as wee here obey
The statecloth where the Prince sate yesterday,
Crants to such brave Loves will not be inthrall'd,
But loves her onely, who at Geneva is call'd
Religion, plaine, simple, sullen, yong,
Contemptuous, yet unhansome. As among

Lecherous humors, there is one that judges
No wenches wholsome, but course country drudges.
Graius stayes still at home here, and because
Some Preachers, vile ambitious bauds, and lawes
Still new like fashions, bid him thinke that shee
Which dwels with us, is onely perfect, hee
Imbraceth her, whom his Godfathers will
Tender to him, being tender, as Wards still
Take such wives as their Guardians offer, or
Pay valewes. Carelesse Phrygius doth abhorre
All, because all cannot be good, as one
Knowing some women whores, dares marry none.
Graccus loves all as one, and thinkes that so
As women do in divers countries goe
In divers habits, yet are still one kinde;
So doth, so is Religion; and this blind-
nesse too much light breeds; but unmoved thou
Of force must one, and forc'd but one allow;
And the right; aske thy father which is shee,
Let him aske his; though truth and falsehood bee
Neare twins, yet truth a little elder is;
Be busie to seeke her, beleeve mee this,
Hee's not of none, nor worst, that seekes the best.
To adore, or scorne an image, or protest,
May all be bad; doubt wisely, in strange way
To stand inquiring right, is not to stray;
To sleepe, or runne wrong, is: on a huge hill,

Cragg'd, and steep, Truth stands, and hee that will
Reach her, about must, and about must goe;
And what the hills suddennes resists, winne so;
Yet strive so, that before age, deaths twilight,
Thy Soule rest, for none can worke in that night.
To will, implyes delay, therefore now doe.
Hard deeds, the bodies paines; hard knowledge too
The mindes indeavours reach, and mysteries
Are like the Sunne, dazzling, yet plaine to all eyes;
Keepe the truth which thou hast found; men do not stand
In so ill case here, that God hath with his hand
Sign'd Kings blanck-charters to kill whom they hate,
Nor are they Vicars, but hangmen to Fate.
Foole and wretch, wilt thou let thy Soule be tyed
To mans lawes, by which she shall not be tryed
At the last day? Will it then boot thee
To say a Philip, or a Gregory,
A Harry, or a Martin taught thee this?
Is not this excuse for mere contraries,
Equally strong? cannot both sides say so?
That thou mayest rightly obey power, her bounds know;
Those past, her nature, and name is chang'd; to be
Then humble to her is idolatrie;
As streames are, Power is; those blest flowers that dwell
At the rough streames calme head, thrive and do well,
But having left their roots, and themselves given
To the streames tyrannous rage, alas are driven

Through mills, and rockes, and woods, and at last, almost
Consum'd in going, in the sea are lost:
So perish Soules, which more chuse mens unjust
Power from God claym'd, then God himselfe to trust.

SATYRE IV

Well; I may now receive, and die; My sinne
Indeed is great, but I have beene in
A Purgatorie, such as fear'd hell is
A recreation, and scant map of this.
My minde, neither with prides itch, nor yet hath been
Poyson'd with love to see, or to bee seene,
I had no suit there, nor new suite to shew,
Yet went to Court; But as Glaze which did goe
To'a Masse in jest, catch'd, was faine to disburse
The hundred markes, which is the Statutes curse,
Before he scapt; So'it pleas'd my destinie
(Guilty of my sin of going), to thinke me
As prone to all ill, and of good as forget-
full, as proud, as lustfull, and as much in debt,
As vaine, as witlesse, and as false as they
Which dwell at Court, for once going that way.
Therefore I suffered this; Towards me did runne
A thing more strange, then on Niles slime, the Sunne
E'r bred, or all which into Noahs Arke came:
A thing, which would have pos'd Adam to name,
Stranger then seaven Antiquaries studies,
Then Africks Monsters, Guianaes rarities,
Stranger then strangers; One, who for a Dane,
In the Danes Massacre had sure beene slaine,
If he had liv'd then; And without helpe dies,

When next the Prentises 'gainst Strangers rise.
One, whom the watch at noone lets scarce goe by,
One, to whom, the examining Justice sure would cry,
Sir, by your priesthood tell me what you are.
His cloths were strange, though coarse; and black,
    though bare;
Sleeveless his jerkin was, and it had beene
Velvet, but 'twas now (so much ground was seene)
Become Tufftaffatie; and our children shall
See it plaine Rashe awhile, then nought at all.
This thing hath travail'd, and saith, speakes all tongues
And only knoweth what to all States belongs.
Made of th'Accents, and best phrase of all these,
He speakes one language; If strange meats displease,
Art can deceive, or hunger force my tast,
But Pedants motley tongue, souldiers bumbast,
Mountebankes drugtongue, nor the termes of law
Are strong enough preparatives, to draw
Me to beare this, yet I must be content
With his tongue: in his tongue, call'd complement:
In which he can win widdowes, and pay scores,
Make men speake treason, cosen subtlest whores,
Out-flatter favorites, or outlie either
Jovius, or Surius, or both together.
He names mee, and comes to mee; I whisper, God!
How have I sinn'd, that thy wraths furious rod,
This fellow chuseth me? He saith, Sir,

I love your judgement; Whom doe you prefer,
For the best linguist? And I seelily
Said, that I thought Calepines Dictionarie;
Nay, but of men, most sweet Sir. Beza then,
Some Jesuites, and two reverend men
Of our two Academies, I named; There
He stopt mee, and said; Nay, your Apostles were
Good pretty linguists, and so Panurge was;
Yet a poore gentleman; all these may passe
By travaile. Then, as if he would have sold
His tongue, he praised it, and such wonders told
That I was faine to say, If you'had liv'd, Sir,
Time enough to have beene Interpreter
To Babells bricklayers, sure the Tower had stood.
He adds, If of court life you knew the good,
You would leave lonenesse; I said, not alone
My lonenesse is, but Spartanes fashion,
To teach by painting drunkards, doth not last
Now; Aretines pictures have made few chast;
No more can Princes courts, though there be few
Better pictures of vice, teach me vertue;
He, like to a high strecht lute string squeakt, O Sir,
'Tis sweet to talke of Kings. At Westminster,
Said I, The man that keepes the Abbey tombes,
And for his price doth with who ever comes,
Of all our Harries, and our Edwards talke,
From King to King and all their kin can walke:

Your eares shall heare nought, but Kings; your eyes meet
Kings only; The way to it, is Kingstreet.
He smack'd, and cry'd, He's base, Mechanique, coarse,
So are all your Englishmen in their discourse.
Are not your Frenchmen neate? Mine? as you see,
I have but one Frenchman, looke, hee followes mee.
Certes they are neatly cloth'd. I, of this minde am,
Your only wearing is your Grogaram.
Not so Sir, I have more. Under this pitch
He would not flie; I chaff'd him; But as Itch
Scratch'd into smart, and as blunt iron ground
Into an edge, hurts worse: So, I (foole) found,
Crossing hurt mee; To fit my sullennesse,
He to another key, his stile doth addresse,
And askes, what newes? I tell him of new playes.
He takes my hand, and as a Still, which staies
A Sembriefe, 'twixt each drop, he nigardly,
As loth to enrich mee, so tells many a lie.
More then ten Hollensheads, or Halls, or Stowes,
Of triviall houshold trash he knowes; He knowes
When the Queene frown'd, or smil'd, and he knowes what
A subtle States-man may gather of that;
He knowes who loves; whom; and who by poyson
Hasts to an Offices reversion;
He knowes who'hath sold his land, and now doth beg
A licence, old iron, bootes, shooes, and egge-
shels to transport; Shortly boyes shall not play

At span-counter, or blow-point, but they pay
Toll to some Courtier; And wiser then all us,
He knowes what Ladie is not painted; Thus
He with home-meats tries me; I belch, spue, spit,
Looke pale, and sickly, like a Patient; Yet
He thrusts on more; And as if he'undertooke
To say Gallo-Belgicus without booke
Speakes of all States, and deeds, that have been since
The Spaniards came, to the losse of Amyens.
Like a bigge wife, at sight of loathed meat,
Readie to travaile: So I sigh, and sweat
To heare this Makeron talke in vaine: For yet,
Either my humour, or his owne to fit,
He like a priviledg'd spie, whom nothing can
Discredit, Libells now 'gainst each great man.
He names a price for every office paid;
He saith, our warres thrive ill, because delai'd;
That offices are entail'd, and that there are
Perpetuities of them, lasting as farre
As the last day; And that great officers,
Doe with the Pirates share, and Dunkirkers.
Who wasts in meat, in clothes, in horse, he notes;
Who loves Whores, who boyes, and who goats.
I more amas'd then Circes prisoners, when
They felt themselves turne beasts, felt my selfe then
Becomming Traytor, and mee thought I saw
One of our Giant Statutes ope his jaw

To sucke me in; for hearing him, I found
That as burnt venome Leachers do grow sound
By giving others their soares, I might growe
Guilty, and he free: Therefore I did shew
All signes of loathing; But since I am in,
I must pay mine, and my forefathers sinne
To the last farthing; Therefore to my power
Toughly and stubbornly I beare this crosse;
      But the'houre
Of mercy now was come; He tries to bring
Me to pay a fine to scape his torturing,
And saies, Sir, can you spare me; I said, willingly;
Nay, Sir, can you spare me a crowne? Thankfully I
Gave it, as Ransome; But as fidlers, still,
Though they be paid to be gone, yet needs will
Thrust one more jigge upon you: so did hee
With his long complementall thankes vexe me.
But he is gone, thankes to his needy want,
And the prerogative of my Crowne: Scant
His thankes were ended, when I, (which did see
All the court fill'd with more strange things then hee)
Ran from thence with such or more haste, then one
Who feares more actions, doth haste from prison;
At home in wholesome solitarinesse
My precious soule began, the wretchednesse
Of suiters at court to mourne, and a trance
Like his, who dreamt he saw hell, did advance

It selfe on mee, Such men as he saw there,
I saw at court, and worse, and more; Low feare
Becomes the guiltie, not the accuser; Then,
Shall I, nones slave, of high borne, or rais'd men
Feare frownes? And, my Mistresse Truth, betray thee
To th'huffing braggart, puft Nobility?
No, no, Thou which since yesterday hast beene
Almost about the whole world, hast thou seene,
O Sunne, in all thy journey, Vanitie,
Such as swells the bladder of our court? I
Thinke he which made your waxen garden, and
Transported it from Italy to stand
With us, at London, flouts our Presence, for
Just such gay painted things, which no sappe, nor
Tast have in them, ours are; And naturall
Some of the stocks are, their fruits, bastard all.
'Tis ten a clock and past; All whom the Mues,
Baloune, Tennis, Dyet, or the stewes,
Had all the morning held, now the second
Time made ready, that day, in flocks, are found
In the Presence, and I, (God pardon mee.)
As fresh, and sweet their Apparrells be, as bee
The fields they sold to buy them; For a King
Those hose are, cry the flatterers; And bring
Them next weeke to the Theatre to sell;
Wants reach all states; Me seemes they doe as well
At stage, as court; All are players, who e'r lookes

(For themselves dare not goe) o'r Cheapside books,
Shall finde their wardrops Inventory; Now,
The Ladies come; As Pirats, which doe know
That there came weak ships fraught with Cutchannel,
The men board them; and praise, as they thinke, well,
Their beauties; they the mens wits; Both are bought.
Why good wits ne'r weare scarlet gownes, I thought
This cause, These men, mens wits for speeches buy,
And women buy all reds which scarlets die.
He call'd her beauty limetwigs, her haire net.
She feares her drugs ill laid, her haire loose set;
Would not Heraclitus laugh to see Macrine,
From hat, to shooe, himselfe at doore refine,
As if the Presence were a Moschite, and lift
His skirts and hose, and call his clothes to shrift,
Making them confesse not only mortall
Great staines and holes in them; but veniall
Feathers and dust, wherewith they fornicate:
And then by *Durers* rules survay the state
Of his each limbe, and with strings the odds trye
Of his neck to his legge, and wast to thighes.
So in immaculate clothes, and Symetrie
Perfect as circles, with such nicetie
As a young Preacher at his first time goes
To preach, he enters, and a Lady which owes
Him not so much as good will, he arrests,
And unto her protests protests protests

So much as at Rome would serve to have throwne
Ten Cardinalls into the Inquisition;
And whispered by Jesu, so often, that A
Pursevant would have ravish'd him away
For saying of our Ladies psalter; But 'tis fit
That they each other plague, they merit it.
But here comes Glorius that will plague them both,
Who, in the other extreme, only doth
Call a rough carelessenesse, good fashion;
Whose cloak his spurres teare; whom he spits on
He cares not, His ill words doe no harme
To him; he rusheth in, as if arme, arme,
He meant to crie; And though his face be as ill
As theirs which in old hangings whip Christ, still
He strives to looke worse, he keepes all in awe;
Jeasts like a licenc'd foole, commands like law.
Tyr'd, now I leave this place, and but pleas'd so
As men which from gaoles to'execution goe,
Goe through the great chamber (why is it hung
With the seaven deadly sinnes?) being among
Those Askaparts, men big enough to throw
Charing Crosse for a barre, men that doe know
No token of worth, but Queenes man, and fine
Living, barrells of beefe, flaggons of wine;
I shooke like a spyed Spie; Preachers which are
Seas of Wits and Arts, you can, then dare,
Drowne the sinnes of this place, for, for mee

Which am but a scarce brooke, it enough shall bee
To wash the staines away; though I yet
With *Macchabees* modestie, the knowne merit
Of my worke lessen: yet some wise man shall,
I hope, esteeme my writs Canonicall.

SATYRE V

Thou shalt not laugh in this leafe, Muse, nor they
Whom any pitty warmes; He which did lay
Rules to make Courtiers, (hee being understood
May make good Courtiers, but who Courtiers good?)
Frees from the sting of jests all who in extreme
Are wreched or wicked: of these two a theame
Charity and liberty give me. What is hee
Who Officers rage, and Suiters misery
Can write, and jest? If all things be in all,
As I thinke, since all, which were, are, and shall
Bee, be made of the same elements:
Each thing, each thing implyes or represents.
Then man is a world; in which, Officers
Are the vast ravishing seas; and Suiters,
Springs; now full, now shallow, now drye; which, to
That which drownes them, run: These selfe reasons do
Prove the world a man, in which, officers
Are the devouring stomacke, and Suiters
The excrements, which they voyd; all men are dust;
How much worse are Suiters, who to mens lust
Are made preyes. O worse then dust, or wormes meat
For they do eate you now, whose selves wormes shall eate.
They are the mills which grinde you, yet you are
The winde which drives them; and a wastfull warre
Is fought against you, and you fight it; they

108

Adulterate lawe, and you prepare their way
Like wittals, th'issue your owne ruine is;
Greatest and fairest Empresse, know you this?
Alas, no more then Thames calme head doth know
Whose meades her armes drowne, or whose corne o'rflow:
You Sir, whose righteousness she loves, whom I
By having leave to serve, am most richly
For service paid, authorized, now beginne
To know and weed out this enormous sinne.
O Age of rusty iron! Some better wit
Call it some worse name, if ought equall it;
The iron Age *that* was, when justice was sold, now
Injustice is sold dearer farre; allow
All demands, fees, and duties; gamsters, anon
The mony which you sweat, and sweare for, is gon
Into other hands: So controverted lands
Scape, like Angelica, the strivers hands.
If Law be the Judges heart, and hee
Have no heart to resist letter, or fee,
Where wilt thou appeale? powre of the Courts below
Flow from the first maine head, and these can throw
Thee, if they sucke thee in, to misery,
To fetters, halters; But if the injury
Steele thee to dare complaine, Alas, thou goest
Against the stream, when upwards: when thou art most
Heavy and most faint; and in these labours they,
'Gainst whom thou should'st complaine, will in the way

Become great seas, o'r which, when thou shalt bee
Forc'd to make golden bridges, thou shalt see
That all thy gold was drown'd in them before;
All things follow their like, only who have may have more.
Judges are Gods; he who made and said them so,
Meant not that men should be forc'd to them to goe,
By meanes of Angels; When supplications
We send to God, to Dominations,
Powers, Cherubins, and all heavens Courts, if wee
Should pay fees as here, Daily bread would be
Scarce to Kings; so 'tis. Would it not anger
A Stoicke, a coward, yea a Martyr,
To see a Pursivant come in, and call
All his cloathes, Copes; Bookes, Primers; and all
His Plate, Challices; and mistake them away,
And aske a fee for comming? Oh, ne'r may
Faire lawes white reverend name be strumpeted,
To warrant thefts: she is established
Recorder to Destiny, on earth, and shee
Speakes Fates words, and but tells us who must bee
Rich, who poore, who in chaires, who in jayles:
Shee is all faire, but yet hath foule long nailes,
With which she scracheth Suiters; In bodies
Of men, so in law, nailes are th'extremities,
So Officers stretch to more then Law can doe,
As our nailes reach what no else part comes to.
Why barest thou to yon Officer? Foole, Hath hee

Got those goods, for which erst men bared to thee?
Foole, twice, thrice, thou hast bought wrong, and now
   hungerly
Beg'st right; But that dole comes not till these dye.
Thou had'st much, and lawes Urim and Thummim trie
Thou wouldst for more; and for all hast paper
Enough to cloath all the great Carricks Pepper.
Sell that, and by that thou much more shalt leese,
Then Haman, when he sold his Antiquities.
O wretch that thy fortunes should moralize
Esops fables, and make tales, prophesies.
Thou art the swimming dog whom shadows cosened,
And div'st, neare drowning, for what vanished.

LETTERS TO THE
COUNTESS OF BEDFORD

REASON IS OUR SOULES LEFT HAND

MADAME,
Reason is our Soules left hand, Faith her right,
By these wee reach divinity, that's you;
Their loves, who have the blessings of your light,
Grew from their reason, mine from faire faith grew.

But as, although a squint lefthandednesse
Be'ungracious, yet we cannot want that hand,
So would I, not to encrease, but to expresse
My faith, as I beleeve, so understand.

Therefore I study you first in your Saints,
Those friends, whom your election glorifies,
Then in your deeds, accesses, and restraints,
And what you reade, and what your selfe devize.

But soone, the reasons why you'are lov'd by all,
Grow infinite, and so passe reasons reach,
Then backe againe to'implicate faith I fall,
And rest on what the Catholique voice doth teach;

That you are good: and not one Heretique
Denies it: if he did, yet you are so.
For, rockes, which high top'd and deep rooted sticke,
Waves wash, not undermine, nor overthrow.

In every thing there naturally growes
A *Balsamum* to keepe it fresh, and new,
If'twere not injur'd by extrinsique blowes:
Your birth and beauty are this Balme in you.

But you of learning and religion,
And vertue,'and such ingredients, have made
A methridate, whose operation
Keepes off, or cures what can be done or said.

Yet, this is not your physicke, but your food,
A dyet fit for you; for you are here
The first good Angell, since the worlds frame stood,
That ever did in womans shape appeare.

Since you are then Gods masterpeece, and so
His Factor for our loves; do as you doe,
Make your returne home gracious; and bestow
This life on that; so make one life of two.
    For so God helpe mee,'I would not misse you there
    For all the good which you can do me here.

YOU HAVE REFIN'D MEE

MADAME,
You have refin'd mee, and to worthyest things
Vertue, Art, Beauty, Fortune, now I see
Rarenesse, or use, not nature value brings;
And such, as they are circumstanc'd, they bee.
    Two ills can ne're perplexe us, sinne to'excuse;
    But of two good things, we may leave and chuse.

Therefore at Court, which is not vertues clime,
Where a transcendent height, (as, lownesse mee)
Makes her not be, or not show: all my rime
Your vertues challenge, which there rarest bee;
    For, as darke texts need notes: there some must bee
    To usher vertue, and say, *This is shee.*

So in the country'is beauty; to this place
You are the season (Madame) you the day,
'Tis but a grave of spices, till your face
Exhale them, and a thick close bud display.
    Widow'd and reclus'd else, her sweets she'enshrines
    As China, when the Sunne at Brasill dines.

Out from your chariot, morning breaks at night,
And falsifies both computations so;
Since a new world doth rise here from your light,
We your new creatures, by new recknings goe.
    This showes that you from nature lothly stray,
    That suffer not an artificiall day.

In this you'have made the Court the Antipodes,
And will'd your Delegate, the vulgar Sunne,
To doe profane autumnall offices,
Whilst here to you, wee sacrificers runne;
    And whether Priests, or Organs, you wee'obey,
    We sound your influence, and your Dictates say.

Yet to that Deity which dwels in you,
Your vertuous Soule, I now not sacrifice;
These are *Petitions*, and not *Hymnes*; they sue
But that I may survay the edifice.
    In all Religions as much care hath bin
    Of Temples frames, and beauty,'as Rites within.

As all which goe to Rome, doe not thereby
Esteeme religions, and hold fast the best,
But serve discourse, and curiosity,
With that which doth religion but invest,
    And shunne th'entangling laborinths of Schooles,
    And make it wit, to thinke the wiser fooles:

So in this pilgrimage I would behold
You as you'are vertues temple, not as shee,
What walls of tender christall her enfold,
What eyes, hands, bosome, her pure Altars bee;
    And after this survay, oppose to all
    Bablers of Chappels, you th'Escuriall.

Yet not as consecrate, but merely'as faire;
On these I cast a lay and country eye.
Of past and future stories, which are rare
I finde you all record, and prophecie.
    Purge but the booke of Fate, that it admit
    No sad nor guilty legends, you are it.

If good and lovely were not one, of both
You were the transcript, and originall,
The Elements, the Parent, and the Growth,
And every peece of you, is both their All,
    So'intire are all your deeds, and you, that you
    Must do the same thinge still; you cannot two.

But these (as nice thinne Schoole divinity
Serves heresie to furder or represse)
Tast of Poëtique rage, or flattery,
And need not, where all hearts one truth professe;
    Oft from new proofes, and new phrase, new doubts grow,
    As strange attire aliens the men wee know.

Leaving then busie praise, and all appeale,
To higher Courts, senses decree is true,
The Mine, the Magazine, the Commonweale,
The story of beauty,'in Twicknam is, and you.
   Who hath seene one, would both; As, who had bin
   In Paradise, would seeke the Cherubin.

T'HAVE WRITTEN THEN

T'have written then, when you writ, seem'd to mee
    Worst of spirituall vices, Simony,
And not t'have written then, seemes little lesse
    Then worst of civill vices, thanklessenesse.
In this, my debt I seem'd loath to confesse,
    In that, I seem'd to shunne beholdingnesse.
But 'tis not soe, *nothings*, as I am, may
    Pay all they have, and yet have all to pay.
Such borrow in their payments, and owe more
    By having leave to write so, then before.
Yet since rich mines in barren grounds are showne,
    May not I yeeld (not gold) but coale or stone?
Temples were not demolish'd, though prophane:
    Here *Peter Joves*, there *Paul* hath Dian's Fane.
So whether my hymnes you admit or chuse,
    In me you'have hallowed a Pagan Muse,
And denizend a stranger, who mistaught
    By blamers of the times they mard, hath sought
Vertues in corners, which now bravely doe
    Shine in the worlds best part, or all It; You.
I have been told, that vertue'in Courtiers hearts
    Suffers an Ostracisme, and departs.
Profit, ease, fitnesse, plenty, bid it goe,
    But whither, only knowing you, I know;
Your (or you) vertue two vast uses serves,

It ransomes one sex, and one Court preserves;
There's nothing but your worth, which being true,
   Is knowne to any other, not to you.
And you can never know it; To admit
   No knowledge of your worth, is some of it.
But since to you, your praises discords bee,
   Stoop, others ills to meditate with mee.
Oh! to confesse wee know not what we should,
   Is halfe excuse, wee know not what we would.
Lightnesse depresseth us, emptinesse fills,
   We sweat and faint, yet still goe downe the hills;
As new Philosophy arrests the Sunne,
   And bids the passive earth about it runne,
So wee have dull'd our minde, it hath no ends;
   Onely the bodie's busie, and pretends;
As dead low earth ecclipses and controules
   The quick high Moone: so doth the body, Soules.
In none but us, are such mixt engines found,
   As hands of double office: For, the ground
We till with them; and them to heav'n wee raise;
   Who prayer-lesse labours, or, without this, prayes,
Doth but one halfe, that's none; He which said, *Plough*
   And looke not back, to looke up doth allow.
Good seed degenerates, and oft obeys
   The soyles disease, and into cockle strayes.
Let the minds thoughts be but transplanted so,
   Into the body,'and bastardly they grow.

What hate could hurt our bodies like our love?
  Wee but no forraine tyrans could remove,
These not ingrav'd, but inborne dignities,
  Caskets of soules; Temples, and Palaces:
For, bodies shall from death redeemed bee,
  Soules but preserv'd, not naturally free;
As men to'our prisons, new soules to us are sent,
  Which learne vice there, and come in innocent.
First seeds of every creature are in us,
  What ere the world hath bad, or pretious,
Mans body can produce, hence hath it beene
    That stones, wormes, frogges, and snakes in man
        are seene.
But who ere saw, though nature can worke soe,
  That pearle, or gold, or corne in man did grow?
We'have added to the world Virginia,'and sent
  Two new starres lately to the firmament;
Why grudge wee us (not heaven) the dignity
  T'increase with ours, those faire soules company.
But I must end this letter, though it doe
  Stand on two truths, neither is true to you.
Vertue hath some perversenesse; For she will
  Neither beleeve her good, nor others ill.
Even in you, vertues best paradise,
  Vertue hath some, but wise degrees of vice
Too many vertues, or too much of one
  Begets in you unjust suspition.

And ignorance of vice, makes vertue lesse,
  Quenching compassion of our wretchednesse.
But these are riddles; Some aspersion
  Of vice becomes well some complexion.
Statesmen purge vice with vice, and may corrode
  The bad with bad, a spider with a toad:
For so, ill thralls not them, but they tame ill
  And make her do much good against her will,
But in your Commonwealth or world in you
  Vice hath no office, or good worke to doe.
Take then no vitious purge, but be content
With cordiall vertue, your knowne nourishment.

THIS TWILIGHT OF TWO YEARES
To the Countesse of Bedford. On New-yeares day.

This twilight of two yeares, not past nor next,
    Some embleme is of mee, or I of this,
Who Meteor-like, of stuffe and forme perplext,
    Whose *what*, and *where*, in disputation is,
    If I should call mee *any thing*, should misse.

I summe the yeares, and mee, and finde mee not
    Debtor to th'old, nor Creditor to th'new,
That cannot say, My thankes I have forgot,
    Nor trust I this with hopes, and yet scarce true,
    This bravery is since these times shew'd mee you.

In recompence I would show future times
    What you were, and teach them to'urge towards
        such.
Verse embalmes vertue;'and Tombs, or Thrones of
        rimes,
    Preserve fraile transitory fame, as much
    As spice doth bodies from corrupt aires touch.

Mine are short-liv'd; the tincture of your name
    Creates in them, but dissipates as fast,
New spirits: for, strong agents with the same
    Force that doth warme and cherish, us doe wast;
    Kept hot with strong extracts, no bodies last:

So, my verse built of your just praise, might want
    Reason and likelihood, the firmest Base,
And made of miracle, now faith is scant,
    Will vanish soone, and so possesse no place,
    And you, and it, too much grace might disgrace.

When all (as truth commands assent) confesse
    All truth of you, yet they will doubt how I
One corne of one low anthills dust, and lesse,
    Should name, know, or expresse a thing so high,
    And not an inch, measure infinity.

I cannot tell them, nor my selfe, nor you,
    But leave, lest truth b'endanger'd by my praise,
And turne to God, who knowes I thinke this true,
    And useth oft, when such a heart mis-sayes,
    To make it good, for, such a praiser prayes.

Hee will best teach you, how you should lay out
    His stock of *beauty, learning, favour, blood;*
He will perplex security with doubt,
    And cleare those doubts; hide from you,'and shew
        you good,
    And so increase your appetite and food;

Hee will teach you, that good and bad have not
    One latitude in cloysters, and in Court;
Indifferent there the greatest space hath got;
    Some pitty'is not good there, some vaine disport,
    On this side, sinne with that place may comport.

Yet he, as hee bounds seas, will fixe your houres,
    Which pleasure, and delight may not ingresse,
And though what none else lost, be truliest yours,
    Hee will make you, what you did not, possesse,
    By using others, not vice, but weakenesse.

He will make you speake truths, and credibly,
    And make you doubt, that others doe not so:
Hee will provide you keyes, and locks, to spie,
    And scape spies, to good ends, and hee will show
    What you may not acknowledge, what not know.

For your owne conscience, he gives innocence,
    But for your fame, a discreet warinesse,
And though to scape, then to revenge offence
    Be better, he showes both, and to represse
    Joy, when your state swells, *sadnesse* when'tis lesse.

From need of teares he will defend your soule,
    Or make a rebaptizing of one teare;
Hee cannot, (that's, he will not) dis-inroule
    Your name; and when with active joy we heare
    This private Ghospell, then'tis our New Yeare.

HONOUR IS SO SUBLIME PERFECTION

Honour is so sublime perfection,
And so refinde; that when God was alone
And creaturelesse at first, himselfe had none;

But as of the elements, these which wee tread,
Produce all things with which wee'are joy'd or fed,
And, those are barren both above our head:

So from low persons doth all honour flow;
Kings, whom they would have honoured, to us show,
And but *direct* our honour, not *bestow*.

For when from herbs the pure part must be wonne
From grosse, by Stilling, this is better done
By despis'd dung, then by the fire or Sunne.

Care not then, Madame,'how low your praysers lye;
In labourers balads oft more piety
God findes, then in *Te Deums* melodie.

And, ordinance rais'd on Towers so many mile
Send not their voice, nor last so long a while
As fires from th'earths low vaults in *Sicil* Isle

Should I say I liv'd darker then were true,
Your radiation can all clouds subdue,
But one, 'tis best light to contemplate you.

You, for whose body God made better clay,
Or tooke Soules stuffe such as shall late decay,
Or such as needs small change at the last day.

This, as an Amber drop enwraps a Bee,
Covering discovers your quicke Soule; that we
May in your through-shine front your hearts thoughts
    see.

You teach (though wee learne not) a thing unknowne
To our late times, the use of specular stone,
Through which all things within without were shown.

Of such were Temples; so and such you are;
Beeing and *seeming* is your equall care,
And *vertues* whole *summe* is but *know* and *dare*.

But as our Soules of growth and Soules of sense
Have birthright of our reasons Soule, yet hence
They fly not from that, nor seeke presidence:

Natures first lesson, so discretion,
Must not grudge zeale a place, nor yet keepe none,
Not banish it selfe, nor religion.

Discretion is a wisemans Soule, and so
Religion is a Christians, and you know
How these are one, her *yea*, is not her *no*.

Nor may we hope to sodder still and knit
These two, and dare to breake them; nor must wit
Be colleague to religion, but be it.

In those poor types of God (round circles) so
Religious tipes, the peecelesse centers flow,
And are in all the lines which always goe.

If either ever wrought in you alone
Or principally, then religion
Wrought your ends, and your wayes discretion.

Goe thither stil, goe the same way you went,
Who so would change, do covet or repent;
Neither can reach you, great and innocent.

THOUGH I BE DEAD

Though I be *dead*, and buried, yet I have
   (Living in you,) Court enough in my grave,
As oft as there I thinke my selfe to bee,
   So many resurrections waken mee.
That thankfullnesse your favours have begot
   In mee, embalmes mee, that I doe not rot;
This season as 'tis Easter, as 'tis spring,
   Must both to growth and to confession bring
My thoughts dispos'd unto your influence, so,
   These verses bud, so these confessions grow;
First I confesse I have to others lent
   Your stock, and over prodigally spent
Your treasure, for since I had never knowne
   Vertue or beautie, but as they are growne
In you, I should not thinke or say they shine,
   (So as I have) in any other Mine;
Next I confesse this my confession,
   For, 'tis some fault thus much to touch upon
Your praise to you, where half rights seeme too much,
   And make your minds sincere complexion blush.
Next I confesse my'impertinence, for I
   Can scarce repent my first fault, since thereby
Remote low Spirits, which shall ne'r read you,
   May in lesse lessons finde enough to doe,
By studying copies, not Originals,
       Desunt cætera.

THE FIRST
ANNIVERSARY

When that rich soule which to her Heaven is gone,
Whom all they celebrate, who know they have one,
(For who is sure he hath a soule, unlesse
It see, and Judge, and follow worthinesse,
And by Deedes praise it? He who doth not this,
May lodge an In-mate soule, but tis not his.)
When that Queene ended here her progresse time,
And, as t'her standing house, to heaven did clymbe,
Where, loth to make the Saints attend her long,
Shee's now a part both of the Quire, and Song,
This world, in that great earth-quake languished;
For in a common Bath of teares it bled,
Which drew the strongest vitall spirits out:
But succour'd then with a perplexed doubt,
Whether the world did loose or gaine in this,
(Because since now no other way there is
But goodnes, to see her, whom all would see,
All must endeavour to be good as shee,)
This great consumption to a fever turn'd,
And so the world had fits; it joy'd, it mourn'd.
And, as men thinke, that Agues physicke are,
And th'Ague being spent, give over care,
So thou, sicke world, mistak'st thy selfe to bee
Well, when alas, thou'rt in a Letargee.
Her death did wound, and tame thee than, and than

Thou mightst have better spar'd the Sunne, or Man;
That wound was deepe, but 'tis more misery,
That thou hast lost thy sense and memory.
T'was heavy then to heare thy voyce of mone,
But this is worse, that thou are speechlesse growne.
Thou hast forgot thy name, thou hadst; thou wast
Nothing but she, and her thou hast o'rpast.
For as a child kept from the Font, untill
A Prince, expected long, come to fulfill
The Ceremonies, thou unnam'd hadst laid,
Had not her comming, thee her Palace made:
Her name defin'd thee, gave thee forme and frame,
And thou forgetst to celebrate thy name.
Some moneths she hath beene dead (but being dead,
Measures of times are all determined)
But long shee'ath beene away, long, long, yet none
Offers to tell us who it is that's gone.
But as in states doubtfull of future heyres,
When sickenes without remedy, empayres
The present Prince, they're loth it should be said,
The Prince doth languish, or the Prince is dead:
So mankind feeling now a generall thaw,
A strong example gone equall to law,
The Cyment which did faithfully compact
And glue all vertues, now resolv'd, and slack'd,
Thought it some blasphemy To say sh'was dead;
Or that our weakenes was discovered

In that confession; therefore spoke no more
Then tongues, the soule being gone, the losse deplore.
But though it be too late to succour thee,
Sicke world, yea dead, yea putrified, since shee
Thy'ntrinsique Balme, and thy preservative,
Can never be renew'd, thou never live,
I (since no man can make thee live) will trie,
What we may gaine by thy Anatomy.
Her death hath taught us dearely, that thou art
Corrupt and mortall in thy purest part.
Let no man say, the world it selfe being dead,
'Tis labour lost to have discovered
The worlds infirmities, since there is none
Alive to study this dissectione;
For there's a kind of world remaining still,
Though shee which did inanimate and fill
The world, be gone, yet in this last long night,
Her Ghost doth walke; that is, a glimmering light,
A faint weake love of vertue and of good
Reflects from her, on them which understood
Her worth; And though she have shut in all day,
The twi-light of her memory doth stay;
Which, from the carcasse of the old world, free,
Creates a new world; and new creatures be
Produc'd. The matter and the stuffe of this,
Her vertue, and the forme our practice is.
And though to be thus Elemented, arme

These Creatures, from hom-borne intrinsique harme,
(For all assum'd unto this Dignitee,
So many weedlesse Paradises bee,
Which of themselves produce no venemous sinne,
Except some forraine Serpent bring it in)
Yet, because outward stormes the strongest breake,
And strength it selfe by confidence growes weake,
This new world may be safer, being told
The dangers and diseases of the old:
For with due temper men do then forgoe,
Or covet things, when they their true worth know.
There is no health; Physitians say that we
At best, enjoy, but a neutralitee.
And can there be worse sicknesse, then to know
That we are never well, nor can be so?
We are borne ruinous: poore mothers crie,
That children come not right, nor orderly,
Except they headlong come, and fall upon
An ominous precipitation.
How witty's ruine? how importunate
Upon mankinde? It labour'd to frustrate
Even Gods purpose; and made woman, sent
For mans reliefe, cause of his languishment.
They were to good ends, and they are so still,
But accessory, and principall in ill.
For that first mariage was our funerall:
One woman at one blow, then kill'd us all,

And singly, one by one, they kill us now.
We doe delightfully our selves allow
To that consumption; and profusely blinde,
We kill our selves, to propagate our kinde.
And yet we doe not that; we are not men:
There is not now that mankinde, which was then
When as the Sunne, and man, did seeme to strive,
(Joynt tenants of the world) who should survive.
When Stag, and Raven, and the long-liv'd tree,
Compar'd with man, dy'de in minoritee.
When, if a slow-pac'd starre had stolne away
From the observers marking, he might stay
Two or three hundred yeares to see't againe,
And then make up his observation plaine;
When, as the age was long, the sise was great:
Mans growth confess'd, and recompenc'd the meat:
So spacious and large, that every soule
Did a faire Kingdome, and large Realme controule:
And when the very stature thus erect,
Did that soule a good way towards Heaven direct.
Where is this mankind now? who lives to age,
Fit to be made *Methusalem* his page?
Alas, we scarse live long enough to trie
Whether a new made clocke runne right, or lie.
Old Grandsires talke of yesterday with sorrow,
And for our children we reserve to morrow.
So short is life, that every peasant strives,

In a torne house, or field, to have three lives.
And as in lasting, so in length is man
Contracted to an inch, who was a span.
For had a man at first, in Forrests stray'd,
Or shipwrack'd in the Sea, one would have laid
A wager that an Elephant or Whale
That met him, would not hastily assaile
A thing so equall to him: now alas,
The Fayries, and the Pigmies well may passe
As credible; mankind decayes so soone,
We're scarse our Fathers shadowes cast at noone.
Onely death addes t'our length: nor are we growne
In stature to be men, till we are none.
But this were light, did our lesse volume hold
All the old Text; or had we chang'd to gold
Their silver; or dispos'd into lesse glas,
Spirits of vertue, which then scattred was.
But 'tis not so: w'are not retir'd, but dampt;
And as our bodies, so our mindes are cramp't:
'Tis shrinking, not close-weaving, that hath thus,
In minde and body both bedwarfed us.
We seeme ambitious, Gods whole worke t'undoe;
Of nothing he made us, and we strive too,
To bring our selves to nothing backe; and we
Do what we can, to do't so soone as hee.
With new diseases on our selves we warre,
And with new phisicke, a worse Engin farre.

Thus man, this worlds Vice-Emperor, in whom
All faculties, all graces are at home;
And if in other Creatures they appeare,
They're but mans ministers, and Legats there,
To worke on their rebellions, and reduce
Them to Civility, and to mans use.
This man, whom God did wooe, and loth t'attend
Till man came up, did downe to man descend,
This man, so great, that all that is, is his,
Oh what a trifle, and poore thing he is!
If man were any thing, he's nothing now:
Helpe, or at least some time to wast, allow
T'his other wants, yet when he did depart
With her, whom we lament, he lost his hart.
She, of whom th'Auncients seem'd to prophesie,
When they call'd vertues by the name of shee;
She in whom vertue was so much refin'd,
That for Allay unto so pure a minde
Shee tooke the weaker Sex, she that could drive
The poysonous tincture, and the stayne of *Eve*,
Out of her thoughts, and deeds; and purifie
All, by a true religious Alchimy;
Shee, shee is dead; shee's dead: when thou knowest this,
Thou knowest how poore a trifling thing man is.
And learn'st thus much by our Anatomee,
The heart being perish'd, no part can be free.
And that except thou feed (not banquet) on

The supernaturall food, Religion,
Thy better Grouth growes withered, and scant;
Be more then man, or thou'rt lesse then an Ant.
Then, as mankinde, so is the worlds whole frame
Quite out of joynt, almost created lame:
For, before God had made up all the rest,
Corruption entred, and deprav'd the best:
It seis'd the Angels, and then first of all
The world did in her Cradle take a fall,
And turn'd her braines, and tooke a generall maime
Wronging each joynt of th'universall frame.
The noblest part, man, felt it first; and than
Both beasts and plants, curst in the curse of man.
So did the world from the first houre decay,
The evening was beginning of the day,
And now the Springs and Sommers which we see,
Like sonnes of women after fifty bee.
And new Philosophy cals all in doubt,
The Element of fire is quite put out;
The Sun is lost, and th'earth, and no mans wit
Can well direct him, where to looke for it.
And freely men confesse, that this world's spent,
When in the Planets, and the Firmament
They seeke so many new; they see that this
Is crumbled out againe to his Atomis.
'Tis all in pieces, all cohærence gone;
All just supply, and all Relation:

Prince, Subject, Father, Sonne, are things forgot,
For every man alone thinkes he hath got
To be a Phœnix, and that there can bee
None of that kinde, of which he is, but hee.
This is the worlds condition now, and now
She that should all parts to reunion bow,
She that had all Magnetique force alone,
To draw, and fasten sundred parts in one;
She whom wise nature had invented then
When she observ'd that every sort of men
Did in their voyage in this worlds Sea stray,
And needed a new compasse for their way;
Shee that was best, and first originall
Of all faire copies; and the generall
Steward to Fate; shee whose rich eyes, and brest,
Guilt the West Indies, and perfum'd the East;
Whose having breath'd in this world, did bestow
Spice on those Isles, and bad them still smell so,
And that rich Indie which doth gold interre,
Is but as single money, coyn'd from her:
She to whom this world must it selfe refer,
As Suburbs, or the Microcosme of her,
Shee, shee is dead; shee's dead: when thou knowst this,
Thou knowst how lame a cripple this world is.
And learnst thus much by our Anatomy,
That this worlds generall sickenesse doth not lie
In any humour, or one certaine part;

But, as thou sawest it rotten at the hart,
Thou seest a Hectique fever hath got hold
Of the whole substance, not to be contrould,
And that thou hast but one way, not t'admit
The worlds infection, to be none of it.
For the worlds subtilst immateriall parts
Feele this consuming wound, and ages darts.
For the worlds beauty is decayd, or gone,
Beauty, that's colour, and proportion.
We thinke the heavens enjoy their Spherical
Their round proportion embracing all.
But yet their various and perplexed course,
Observ'd in divers ages doth enforce
Men to finde out so many Eccentrique parts,
Such divers downe-right lines, such overthwarts,
As disproportion that pure forme. It teares
The Firmament in eight and fortie sheeres,
And in those constellations there arise
New starres, and old do vanish from our eyes:
As though heav'n suffred earth-quakes, peace or war,
When new Townes rise, and olde demolish'd are.
They have empayld within a Zodiake
The free-borne Sunne, and keepe twelve signes awake
To watch his steps; the Goat and Crabbe controule,
And fright him backe, who els to eyther Pole,
(Did not these Tropiques fetter him) might runne:
For his course is not round; nor can the Sunne

Perfit a Circle, or maintaine his way
One inche direct; but where he rose to day
He comes no more, but with a cousening line,
Steales by that point, and so is Serpentine:
And seeming weary with his reeling thus,
He meanes to sleepe, being now falne nearer us.
So, of the stares which boast that they do runne
In Circle still, none ends where he begunne.
All their proportion's lame, it sinks, it swels.
For of Meridians, and Parallels,
Man hath weav'd out a net, and this net throwne
Upon the Heavens, and now they are his owne.
Loth to goe up the hill, or labor thus
To goe to heaven, we make heaven come to us.
We spur, we raine the stars, and in their race
They're diversly content t'obey our pace.
But keepes the earth her round proportion still?
Doth not a Tenarif, or higher Hill
Rise so high like a Rocke, that one might thinke
The floating Moone would shipwracke there, and sink?
Seas are so deepe, that Whales being strooke to day,
Perchance to morrow, scarse at middle way
Of their wish'd journeys end, the bottom, dye.
And men, to sound depths, so much line untie,
As one might justly thinke, that there would rise
At end thereof, one of th'Antipodies:
If under all, a Vault infernall be,

(Which sure is spacious, except that we
Invent another torment, that there must
Millions into a strait hote roome be thrust)
Then solidnes, and roundnes have no place.
Are these but warts, and pock-holes in the face
Of th'earth? Thinke so: But yet confesse, in this
The worlds proportion disfigured is,
That those two legges whereon it doth relie,
Reward and punishment are bent awrie.
And, Oh, it can no more be questioned,
That beauties best, proportion, is dead,
Since even griefe it selfe, which now alone
Is left us, is without proportion.
Shee by whose lines proportion should bee
Examin'd, measure of all Symmetree,
Whom had that Ancient seen, who thought soules made
Of Harmony, he would at next have said
That Harmony was shee, and thence infer,
That soules were but Resultances from her,
And did from her into our bodies go,
As to our eyes, the formes from objects flow:
Shee, who if those great Doctors truely said
That th'Arke to mans proportions was made,
Had beene a type for that, as that might be
A type of her in this, that contrary
Both Elements, and Passions liv'd at peace
In her, who caus'd all Civill warre to cease.

Shee, after whom, what forme soe're we see,
Is discord, and rude incongruitee,
Shee, shee is dead; she's dead; when thou knowst this,
Thou knowst how ugly a monster this world is:
And learnst thus much by our Anatomee,
That here is nothing to enamor thee:
And that, not onely faults in inward parts,
Corruptions in our braines, or in our harts,
Poysoning the fountaines, whence our actions spring,
Endanger us: but that if every thing
Be not done fitly'and in proportion,
To satisfie wise, and good lookers on,
(Since most men be such as most thinke they bee)
They're lothsome too, by this Deformitee.
For good, and well, must in our actions meete:
Wicked is not much worse then indiscreet.
But beauties other second Element,
Colour, and lustre now, is as neere spent.
And had the world his just proportion,
Were it a ring still, yet the stone is gone.
As a compassionate Turcoyse which doth tell
By looking pale, the wearer is not well,
As gold fals sicke being stung with Mercury,
All the worlds parts of such complexion bee.
When nature was most busie, the first weeke,
Swadling the new-borne earth, God seemd to like,
That she should sport herselfe sometimes, and play,

To mingle and vary colours every day.
And then, as though she could not make inow,
Himselfe his various Rainbow did allow.
Sight is the noblest sense of any one,
Yet sight hath onely color to feed on,
And color is decayd: summers robe growes
Duskie, and like an oft dyed garment showes.
Our blushing redde, which us'd in cheekes to spred,
Is inward sunke, and onely our soules are redde.
Perchance the world might have recovered,
If she whom we lament had not beene dead:
But shee, in whom all white, and redde, and blue
(Beauties ingredients) voluntary grew,
As in an unvext Paradise; from whom
Did all things verdure, and their lustre come,
Whose composition was miraculous,
Being all colour, all Diaphanous,
(For Ayre, and Fire but thicke grosse bodies were,
And liveliest stones but drowsie, and pale to her,)
Shee, shee is dead; shee's dead: when thou knowst this,
Thou knowst how wan a Ghost this our world is:
And learnst thus much by our Anatomee,
That it should more affright, then pleasure thee.
And that, since all faire colour then did sinke,
Tis now but wicked vanity to thinke,
To color vitious deeds with good pretence,
Or with bought colors to illude mens sense.

Nor in ought more this worlds decay appeares,
Then that her influence the heav'n forbeares,
Or that the Elements doe not feele this,
The father, or the mother barren is.
The clouds conceive not raine, or doe not powre
In the due birth-time, downe the balmy showre.
Th'Ayre doth not motherly sit on the earth,
To hatch her seasons, and give all things birth.
Spring-times were common cradles, but are toombes;
And false-conceptions fill the general wombs.
Th'Ayre showes such Meteors, as none can see,
Not onely what they meane, but what they bee.
Earth such new wormes, as would have troubled much,
Th'Egyptian Mages to have made more such.
What Artist now dares boast that he can bring
Heaven hither, or constellate any thing,
So as the influence of those starres may bee
Imprisond in an Herbe, or Charme, or Tree,
And doe by touch, all which those starres could do?
The art is lost, and correspondence too.
For heaven gives little, and the earth takes lesse,
And man least knowes their trade, and purposes.
If this commerce twixt heaven and earth were not
Embarr'd, and all this trafique quite forgot,
Shee, for whose losse we have lamented thus,
Would worke more fully'and pow'rfully on us.
Since herbes, and roots, by dying, lose not all,

But they, yea Ashes too, are medicinall,
Death could not quench her vertue so, but that
It would be (if not follow'd) wondred at:
And all the world would be one dying Swan,
To sing her funerall prayse, and vanish than.
But as some Serpents poyson hurteth not,
Except it be from the live Serpent shot,
So doth her vertue need her here, to fit
That unto us; she working more then it.
But she, in whom, to such maturity,
Vertue was growne, past growth, that it must die,
She from whose influence all Impressions came,
But, by Receivers impotencies, lame,
Who, though she could not transubstantiate
All states to gold, yet guilded every state,
So that some Princes have some temperance;
Some Counsaylors some purpose to advance
The common profite; and some people have
Some stay, no more then Kings should give, to crave;
Some women have some taciturnity;
Some Nunneries, some graines of chastity.
She that did thus much, and much more could doe,
But that our age was Iron, and rusty too,
Shee, shee is dead; shee's dead: when thou knowst this,
Thou knowst how drie a Cinder this world is.
And learnst thus much by our Anatomy,
That 'tis in vaine to dew, or mollifie

It with thy Teares, or Sweat, or Bloud: no thing
Is worth our travaile, griefe, or perishing,
But those rich joyes, which did possesse her hart,
Of which shee's now partaker, and a part.
But as in cutting up a man that's dead,
The body will not last out to have read
On every part, and therefore men direct
Their speech to parts, that are of most effect;
So the worlds carcasse would not last, if I
Were punctuall in this Anatomy.
Nor smels it well to hearers, if one tell
Them their disease, who faine would think they're wel.
Here therefore be the end: And, blessed maid,
Of whom is meant what ever hath beene said,
Or shall be spoken well by any tongue,
Whose name refines course lines, and makes prose song,
Accept this tribute, and his first yeares rent,
Who till his darke short tapers end be spent,
As oft as thy feast sees this widow'd earth,
Will yearely celebrate thy second birth,
That is, thy death. For though the soule of man
Be got when man is made, 'tis borne but than
When man doth die. Our body's as the wombe,
And as a mid-wife death directs it home.
And you her creatures, whom she workes upon
And have your last, and best concoction
From her example, and her vertue, if you

In reverence to her, doe thinke it due,
That no one should her prayses thus reherse,
As matter fit for Chronicle, not verse,
Vouchsafe to call to minde, that God did make
A last, and lasting peece, a song. He spake
To *Moses* to deliver unto all,
That song: because hee knew they would let fall
The Law, the Prophets, and the History,
But keepe the song still in their memory.
Such an opinion (in due measure) made
Me this great Office boldly to invade.
Nor could incomprehensiblenesse deterre
Me, from thus trying to emprison her.
Which when I saw that a strict grave could do,
I saw not why verse might not doe so too.
Verse hath a middle nature: heaven keepes soules,
The grave keeps bodies, verse the fame enroules.

HOLY SONNETS

HOLY SONNETS
[*Divine Meditations*]

Thou hast made me, And shall thy worke decay?
Repaire me now, for now mine end doth haste,
I runne to death, and death meets me as fast,
And all my pleasures are like yesterday,
I dare not move my dimme eyes any way,
Despaire behind, and death before doth cast
Such terrour, and my feeble flesh doth waste
By sinne in it, which it t'wards hell doth weigh;
Onely thou art above, and when towards thee
By thy leave I can looke, I rise againe;
But our old subtle foe so tempteth me,
That not one houre my selfe I can sustaine,
Thy Grace may wing me to prevent his art,
And thou like Adamant draw mine iron heart.

I am a little world made cunningly
Of Elements, and an Angelike spright,
But black sinne hath betraid to endless night
My worlds both parts, and (oh) both parts must die.
You which beyond that heaven which was most high
Have found new sphears, and of new lands can write,
Powre new seas in mine eyes, that so I might
Drowne my world with my weeping earnestly,
Or wash it if it must be drown'd no more:
But oh it must be burnt; alas the fire
Of lust and envie have burnt it heretofore,
And made it fouler; Let their flames retire,
And burne me ô Lord, with a fiery zeale
Of thee and thy house, which doth in eating heale.

ANNUNCIATION

Salvation to all that will is nigh,
That All, which alwayes is All every where,
Which cannot sinne, and yet all sinnes must beare,
Which cannot die, yet cannot chuse but die,
Loe, faithfull Virgin, yeelds himselfe to lye
In prison, in thy wombe; and though he there
Can take no sinne, nor thou give, yet he'will weare
Taken from thence, flesh, which deaths force may trie.
Ere by the spheares time was created, thou
Wast in his minde, who is thy Sonne, and Brother,
Whom thou conceiv'st, conceiv'd; yea thou art now
Thy Makers maker, and thy Fathers mother,
Thou'hast light in darke; and shutst in little roome,
Immensity cloysterd in thy deare wombe.

NATIVITIE

Immensitie cloysterd in thy deare wombe,
Now leaves his welbelov'd imprisonment,
There he hath made himselfe to his intent
Weake enough, now into our world to come;
But Oh, for thee, for him, hath th'Inne no roome?
Yet lay him in this stall, and from the Orient,
Starres, and wisemen will travell to prevent
Th'effect of *Herods* jealous generall doome;
Seest thou, my Soule, with thy faiths eyes, how he
Which fils all place, yet none holds him, doth lye?
Was not his pity towards thee wondrous high,
That would have need to be pittied by thee?
Kisse him, and with him into Egypt goe,
With his kinde mother, who partakes thy woe.

O might those sighes and teares returne againe
Into my breast and eyes, which I have spent,
That I might in this holy discontent
Mourne with some fruit, as I have mourn'd in vaine;
In mine Idolatry what showres of raine
Mine eyes did waste? what griefs my heart did rent?
That sufferance was my sinne I now repent,
'Cause I did suffer I must suffer paine.
Th'hydroptique drunkard, and night-scouting thiefe,
The itchy Lecher, and selfe tickling proud
Have the remembrance of past joyes, for reliefe
Of comming ills. To (poore) me is allow'd
No ease; for, long, yet vehement griefe hath beene
Th'effect and cause, the punishment and sinne.

This is my playes last scene, here heavens appoint
My pilgrimages last mile; and my race
Idly, yet quickly runne, hath this last pace,
My spans last inch, my minutes latest point,
And gluttonous death, will instantly unjoynt
My body, and soule, and I shall sleepe a space,
But my'ever-waking part shall see that face,
Whose feare already shakes my every joynt:
Then, as my soule, to'heaven her first seate, takes
        flight,
And earth borne body, in the earth shall dwell,
So, fall my sinnes, that all may have their right,
To where they'are bred, and would presse me, to hell.
Impute me righteous, thus purg'd of evill,
For thus I leave the world, the flesh, the devill.

At the round earths imagin'd corners, blow
Your trumpets, Angells, and arise, arise
From death, you numberlesse infinities
Of soules, and to your scattred bodies goe,
All whom the flood did, and fire shall o'erthrow,
All whom warre, dearth, age, agues, tyrannies,
Despaire, law, chance, hath slaine, and you whose eyes,
Shall behold God, and never tast deaths woe,
But let them sleepe, Lord, and mee mourne a space,
For, if above all these, my sinnes abound,
'Tis late to aske abundance of thy grace,
When wee are there; here on this lowly ground,
Teach mee how to repent; for that's as good
As if thou'hadst seal'd my pardon, with thy blood.

Why are wee by all creatures waited on?
Why doe the prodigall elements supply
Life and food to mee, being more pure then I,
Simple, and further from corruption?
Why brook'st thou, ignorant horse, subjection?
Why dost thou bull, and bore so seelily
Dissemble weaknesse, and by'one mans stroke die,
Whose whole kinde, you might swallow and feed
        upon?
Weaker I am, woe is mee, and worse then you,
You have not sinn'd, nor need be timorous,
But wonder at a greater wonder, for to us
Created nature doth these things subdue,
But their Creator, whom sin, nor nature tyed,
For us, his Creatures, and his foes, hath dyed.

What if this present were the worlds last night?
Marke in my heart, O Soule, where thou dost dwell,
The picture of Christ crucified, and tell
Whether his countenance can thee affright,
Teares in his eyes quench the amasing light,
Blood fills his frownes, which from his pierc'd head fell
And can that tongue adjudge thee unto hell,
Which pray'd forgivenesse for his foes fierce spight?
No, no; but as in my idolatrie
I said to all my profane mistresses,
Beauty, of pitty, foulnesse onely is
A signe of rigour: so I say to thee,
To wicked spirits are horrid shapes assign'd,
This beauteous forme assumes a pitious minde.

Batter my heart, three person'd God; for, you
As yet but knocke, breathe, shine, and seeke to mend;
That I may rise, and stand, o'erthrow mee,'and bend
Your force, to breake, blowe, burn and make me new.
I, like an usurpt towne, to'another due,
Labour to'admit you, but Oh, to no end,
Reason your viceroy in mee, mee should defend,
But is captiv'd, and proves weake or untrue,
Yet dearely'I love you,'and would be lov'd faine,
But am betroth'd unto your enemie,
Divorce mee,'untie, or breake that knot againe,
Take mee to you, imprison mee, for I
Except you'enthrall mee, never shall be free,
Nor ever chast, except you ravish mee.

Since she whom I lov'd hath payd her last debt
To Nature, and to hers, and my good is dead,
And her Soule early into heaven ravished,
Wholly on heavenly things my mind is sett.
Here the admyring her my mind did whett
To seeke thee God; so streames do shew their head;
But thou I have found thee, and thou my thirst hast fed,
A holy thirsty dropsy melts mee yett.
But why should I begg more Love, when as thou
Dost wooe my soule for hers; offring all thine:
And dost not only feare least I allow
My Love to Saints and Angels things divine,
But in thy tender jealosy dost doubt
Least the World, Fleshe, yea Devill putt thee out.

Show me deare Christ, thy Spouse, so bright and clear.
What! is it she, which on the other shore
Goes richly painted? or which rob'd and tore
Laments and mournes in Germany and here?
Sleepes she a thousand, then peepes up one yeare?
Is she selfe truth and errs? now new, now outwore?
Doth she, and did she, and shall she evermore
On one, on seaven, or on no hill appeare?
Dwells she with us, or like adventuring knights
First travaile we to seeke and then make Love?
Betray kind husband thy spouse to our sights,
And let myne amorous soule court thy mild Dove,
Who is most trew, and pleasing to thee, then
When she'is embrac'd and open to most men.

Death be not proud, though some have called thee
Mighty and dreadfull, for, thou are not soe,
For, those, whom thou think'st, thou dost overthrow,
Die not, poore death, nor yet canst thou kill mee;
From rest and sleepe, which but thy pictures bee,
Much pleasure, then from thee, much more must flow,
And soonest our best men with thee doe goe,
Rest of their bones, and soules deliverie.
Thou art slave to Fate, chance, kings, and desperate
     men,
And dost with poyson, warre, and sicknesse dwell,
And poppie, or charmes can make us sleepe as well,
And better then thy stroake; why swell'st thou then?
One short sleepe past, wee wake eternally,
And death shall be no more, death, thou shalt die.

DIVINE POEMS

RESURRECTION, IMPERFECT

Sleep sleep old Sun, thou canst not have repast
As yet, the wound thou took'st on friday last;
Sleepe then, and rest; The world may beare thy stay,
A better Sun rose before thee to day,
Who, not content to'enlighten all that dwell
On the earths face, as thou, enlightned hell,
And made the darke fires languish in that vale,
As, at thy presence here, our fires grow pale.
Whose body having walk'd on earth, and now
Hasting to Heaven, would, that he might allow
Himselfe unto all stations, and fill all,
For these three daies become a minerall;
Hee was all gold when he lay downe, but rose
All tincture, and doth not alone dispose
Leaden and iron wills to good, but is
Of power to make even sinfull flesh like his.
Had one of those, whose credulous pietie
Thought, that a Soule one might discerne and see
Goe from a body,'at this sepulcher been,
And, issuing from the sheet, this body seen,
He would have justly thought this body a soule,
If, not of any man, yet of the whole.
                    Desunt cætera.

GOODFRIDAY, 1613.
RIDING WESTWARD

Let mans Soule be a Spheare, and then, in this,
The intelligence that moves, devotion is,
And as the other Spheares, by being growne
Subject to forraigne motion, lose their owne,
And being by others hurried every day,
Scarce in a yeare their naturall forme obey:
Pleasure or businesse, so, our Soules admit
For their first mover, and are whirld by it.
Hence is't, that I am carryed towards the West
This day, when my Soules forme bends towards
  the East.
There I should see a Sunne, by rising set,
And by that setting endlesse day beget;
But that Christ on this Crosse, did rise and fall,
Sinne had eternally benighted all.
Yet dare I'almost be glad, I do not see
That spectacle of too much weight for mee.
Who sees Gods face, that is selfe life, must dye;
What a death were it then to see God dye?
It made his owne Lieutenant Nature shrinke,
It made his footstoole crack, and the Sunne winke.
Could I behold those hands which span the Poles,
And tune all spheares at once pierc'd with those holes?
Could I behold that endlesse height which is

Zenith to us, and our Antipodes,
Humbled below us? or that blood which is
The seat of all our Soules, if not of his,
Made durt of dust, or that flesh which was worne
By God, for his apparell, rag'd, and torne?
If on these things I durst not looke, durst I
Upon his miserable mother cast mine eye,
Who was Gods partner here, and furnish'd thus
Halfe of that Sacrifice, which ransom'd us?
Though these things, as I ride, be from mine eye,
They'are present yet unto my memory,
For that looks towards them; and thou look'st
    towards mee,
O Saviour, as thou hang'st upon the tree;
I turne my backe to thee, but to receive
Corrections, till thy mercies bid thee leave.
O thinke mee worth thine anger, punish mee,
Burne off my rusts, and my deformity,
Restore thine Image, so much, by thy grace,
That thou may'st know mee, and I'll turne my face.

A HYMNE TO CHRIST, AT THE AUTHORS LAST GOING TO GERMANY

In what torne ship soever I embarke,
That ship shall be my embleme of thy Arke;
What sea soever swallow mee, that flood
Shall be to mee an embleme of thy bloode;
Though thou with clouds of anger do disguise
Thy face; yet through that maske I know those eyes,
    Which, though they turne away sometimes,
        They never will despise.

I sacrifice this Iland unto thee,
And all whom I lov'd there, and who lov'd mee;
When I have put our seas twixt them and mee,
Put thou thy sea betwixt my sinnes and thee.
As the trees sap doth seeke the root below
In winter, in my winter now I goe,
    Where none but thee, th'Eternall root
        Of true Love I may know.

Nor thou nor thy religion dost controule,
The amorousnesse of an harmonious Soule,
But thou would'st have that love thy selfe: As thou
Art jealous, Lord, so I am jealous now,
Thou lov'st not, till from loving more, thou free
My soule: Who ever gives, takes libertie:
   O, if thou car'st not whom I love
     Alas, thou lov'st not mee.

Seale then this bill of my Divorce to All,
On whom those fainter beames of love did fall;
Marry those loves, which in youth scattered bee
On Fame, Wit, Hopes (false mistresses) to thee.
Churches are best for Prayer, that have least light:
To see God only, I goe out of sight:
   And to scape stormy dayes, I chuse
     An Everlasting night.

HYMNE TO GOD MY GOD,
IN MY SICKNESSE

Since I am comming to that Holy roome,
  Where, with thy Quire of Saints for evermore,
I shall be made thy Musique; As I come
  I tune the Instrument here at the dore,
  And what I must doe then, thinke here before.

Whilst my Physitians by their love are growne
  Cosmographers, and I their Mapp, who lie
Flat on this bed, that by them may be showne
  That this is my South-west discoverie
  Per fretum febris, by these streights to die,

I joy, that in these straits, I see my West;
  For, those theire currants yeeld returne to none,
What shall my West hurt me? As West and East
  In all flatt Maps (and I am one) are one,
  So death doth touch the Resurrection.

Is the Pacifique Sea my home? Or are
  The Easterne riches? Is *Jerusalem?*
Anyan, and *Magellan*, and *Gibraltare*,
    All streights, and none but streights are wayes to
      them,
    Whether where *Japhet* dwelt, or *Cham*, or *Sem*.

We thinke that *Paradise* and *Calvarie*,
  Christs Crosse, and *Adams* tree, stood in one place;
Looke Lord, and finde both *Adams* met in me;
    As the first *Adams* sweat surrounds my face,
    May the last *Adams* blood my soule embrace.

So, in his purple wrapp'd receive mee Lord,
  By these his thornes give me his other Crowne;
And as to others soules I preach'd thy word,
    Be this my Text, my Sermon to mine owne,
    Therfore that he may raise the Lord throws down.

A HYMNE TO GOD THE FATHER

I.

Wilt thou forgive that sinne where I begunne,
 Which was my sin, though it were done before?
Wilt thou forgive that sinne, through which I runne,
 And do run still: though still I do deplore?
  When thou hast done, thou hast not done,
   For, I have more.

II.

Wilt thou forgive that sinne which I have wonne
 Others to sinne? and, made my sinne their doore?
Wilt thou forgive that sinne which I did shunne
 A yeare, or two: but wallowed in, a score?
  When thou hast done, thou hast not done,
   For I have more.

III.

I have a sinne of feare, that when I have spunne
 My last thred, I shall perish on the shore;
But sweare by thy selfe, that at my death thy sonne
 Shall shine as he shines now, and heretofore;
  And, having done that, Thou hast done,
   I feare no more.

THE LITANIE

I.

The FATHER

Father of Heaven, and him, by whom
It, and us for it, and all else, for us
   Thou madest, and govern'st ever, come
And re-create mee, now growne ruinous:
      My heart is by dejection, clay,
      And by selfe-murder, red.
From this red earth, O Father, purge away
All vicious tinctures, that new fashioned
I may rise up from death, before I'm dead.

II.

The SONNE

O Sonne of God, who seeing two things,
Sinne, and death crept in, which were never made,
   By bearing one, tryed'st with what stings
The other could thine heritage invade;
      O be thou nail'd unto my heart,
      And crucified againe,
Part not from it, though it from thee would part,
But let it be by applying so thy paine,
Drown'd in thy blood, and in thy passion slaine.

III.

The HOLY GHOST

O Holy Ghost, whose temple I
Am, but of mudde walls, and condensed dust,
   And being sacrilegiously
Halfe wasted with youths fires, of pride and lust,
      Must with new stormes be weatherbeat;
      Double in my heart thy flame,
Which let devout sad teares intend; and let
(Though this glasse lanthorne, flesh, do suffer maime)
Fire, Sacrifice, Priest, Altar be the same.

IV.

The TRINITY

O Blessed glorious Trinity,
Bones to Philosophy, but milke to faith,
   Which, as wise serpents, diversly
Most slipperinesse, yet most entanglings hath,
      As you distinguish'd undistinct
      By power, love, knowledge bee,
Give mee a such selfe different instinct
Of these let all mee elemented bee,
Of power, to love, to know, you unnumbred three.

V.

The Virgin MARY

For that faire blessed Mother-maid,
Whose flesh redeem'd us; That she-Cherubin,
   Which unlock'd Paradise, and made
One claime for innocence, and disseiz'd sinne,
      Whose wombe was a strange heav'n for there
      God cloath'd himselfe, and grew,
Our zealous thankes wee poure. As her deeds were
Our helpes, so are her prayers; nor can she sue
In vaine, who hath such title unto you.

VI.

The Angels

And since this life our nonage is,
And wee in Wardship to thine Angels be,
   Native in heavens faire Palaces,
Where we shall be but denizen'd by thee,
      As th'earth conceiving by the Sunne,
      Yeelds faire diversitie,
Yet never knowes which course that light doth run,
So let mee study, that mine actions bee
Worthy their sight, though blinde in how they see.

VII.
The Patriarches

And let thy Patriarches Desire
(Those great Grandfathers of thy Church, which saw
   More in the cloud, then wee in fire,
Whom Nature clear'd more, then us Grace and Law,
      And now in Heaven still pray, that wee
      May use our new helpes right,)
Be sanctified and fructifie in mee;
Let not my minde be blinder by more light
Nor Faith by Reason added, lose her sight.

VIII.
The Prophets

Thy Eagle-sighted Prophets too,
Which were thy Churches Organs, and did sound
   That harmony, which made of two
One law, and did unite, but not confound;
      Those heavenly Poëts which did see
      Thy will, and it expresse
In rythmique feet, in common pray for mee,
That I by them excuse not my excesse
In seeking secrets, or Poëtiquenesse.

IX.
The Apostles

And thy illustrious Zodiacke
Of twelve Apostles, which ingirt this All,
    (From whom whosoever do not take
Their light, to darke deep pits, throw downe, and fall,)
        As through their prayers, thou'hast let mee know
        That their bookes are divine;
May they pray still, and be heard, that I goe
Th'old broad way in applying; O decline
Mee, when my comment would make thy word mine.

X.
The Martyrs

And since thou so desirously
Did'st long to die, that long before thou could'st,
    And long since thou no more could'st dye,
Thou in thy scatter'd mystique body wouldst
        In Abel dye, and ever since
        In thine, let their blood come
To begge for us, a discreet patience
Of death, or of worse life: for Oh, to some
Not to be Martyrs, is a martyrdome.

XI.
The Confessors

Therefore with thee triumpheth there
A Virgin Squadron of white Confessors,
   Whose bloods betroth'd, not marryed were;
Tender'd, not taken by those Ravishers:
      They know, and pray, that wee may know,
      In every Christian
Hourly tempestuous persecutions grow,
Tentations martyr us alive; A man
Is to himselfe a Dioclesian.

XII.
The Virgins

The cold white snowie Nunnery,
Which, as thy mother, their high Abbesse, sent
   Their bodies backe againe to thee,
As thou hadst lent them, cleane and innocent,
      Though they have not obtain'd of thee,
      That or thy Church, or I,
Should keep, as they, our first integrity;
Divorce thou sinne in us, or bid it die,
And call chast widowhead Virginitie.

XIII.

The Doctors

Thy sacred Academie above
Of Doctors, whose paines have unclasp'd, and taught
    Both bookes of life to us (for love
To know thy Scriptures tells us, we are wrought
        In thy other booke) pray for us there
        That what they have misdone
Or mis-said, wee to that may not adhere,
Their zeale may be our sinne. Lord let us runne
Meane waies, and call them stars, but not the Sunne.

PARADOXES AND
PROBLEMS

Paradox 1: That All Things Kill Themselves

To affect, yea to effect their own deaths, all living are importuned. Not by nature only, which perfects them, but by art and education which perfects her. Plants, quickened and inhabited by the most unworthy soul, which therefore neither will nor work, affect an end, a perfection, a death. This they spend their spirits to attain; this attained, they languish and wither. And by how much more they are by man's industry warmed and cherished and pampered, so much the more early they climb to this perfection, this death. And if, between men, not to defend be to kill, what a heinous self-murder is it not to defend the self. This defence because beasts neglect, they kill themselves: because they exceed us in number, strength, and lawless liberty. Yea, of horses, and so of other beasts, they which inherit most courage by being bred of gallantest parents, and by artificial nursing are bettered, will run to their own deaths, neither solicited by spurs, which they need not, nor by honour, which they apprehend not. If then the valiant kill himself, who can excuse the coward? Or how shall man be free from this, since the first man taught us this – except we cannot kill ourselves because he killed us all? Yet lest something should repair this common ruin, we kill daily our bodies with surfeits, and our minds with anguishes. Of our powers, remembering kills our memory. Of affections, lusting our lust. Of virtues, giving kills liberality. And if these things kill themselves, they do it in their best and supreme perfection, for after perfection immediately follows excess, which changes the natures and the names, and makes them not the same things. If then the best things kill themselves soonest (for no perfection endures) and all things labour to this perfection, all travail to their own death. Yea the frame of the whole world (if it were possible for God to be idle) yet because it begun must die. Then in this idleness imagined in God, what could kill the world but itself, since out of it nothing is?

Paradox 6: That the Gifts of the Body are Better than those of the Mind, or of Fortune

I say again that the body makes the mind. Not that it created it a mind, but forms it a good or bad mind. And this mind may be confounded with soul, without any violence or injustice to reason or philosophy. Then our soul (me seems) is enabled by our body, not this by that. My body licenseth my soul to see the world's beauties through mine eyes, to hear pleasant things through mine ears, and affords it apt organs for conveyance of all perceivable delights. But alas my soul cannot make any part, that is not of itself disposed, to see or hear – though without doubt she be as able and as willing to see behind as before. Now if my soul would say that she enables my parts to taste these pleasures, but is herself only delighted with those rich sweetnesses which her inward eye and senses apprehend, she should dissemble. For I feel her often solaced with beauties which she sees through mine eyes, and music which through mine ears she hears. This perfection then my body hath, that it can impart to my mind all her pleasures; and my mind hath this maim, that she can neither teach my indisposed parts her faculties, nor to the parts best disposed show that beauty of angels or music of spheres, whereof she boasts the contemplation. Are chastity, temperance or fortitude gifts of the mind? I appeal to physicians whether the cause of these be not in the body. Health is a gift of the body, and patience in sickness of the mind. Then who will say this patience is as good a happiness as health, when we must be extremely miserable to have this happiness? And for nourishing of civil societies and mutual love amongst men, which is one chief end why we are men, I say the beauty, proportion and presence of the body hath a more masculine force in begetting this love than the virtues of the mind. For it strikes us suddenly, and possesseth us immediately, when to know these virtues requires sound judgment in him which shall discern, and a long trial and conversation between them. And even at last, alas, how much of our faith and belief shall we be driven to bestow, to assure ourselves that these virtues are not counterfeited? For it is the same to be and to seem virtuous. Because he that hath no virtue can dissemble none. But he that hath a little may gilt and enamel, yea, and transform much vice into virtue. For allow a man to be discreet and flexible to companies – which are great virtues and gifts of the mind – this discretion will be to him the soul and elixir of all virtue. So that, touched with this, even pride shall be made civil humility, and cowardice, honourable and wise valour. But in things seen there is not this danger. For the body which thou lovest and esteemest fair is fair certainly, and if it be not fair in perfection, yet it is fair in the same degree that thy judgment is good. And in a fair body I do seldom suspect a disproportioned mind, or expect a good in a deformed. As when I see a goodly house I assure myself of a worthy possessor, and from a ruinous, withered building I turn away, because it seems either stuffed with varlets, as a prison, or handled by an unworthy negligent tenant, that so suffereth the waste thereof. And truly the gifts of fortune which are riches are only handmaids, yea pandars of the body's pleasure. With their service we nourish health and preserve beauty, and we buy delights. So that virtue which must be loved for herself, and respects no further end, is indeed nothing; and riches, whose end is the good of the body, cannot be so perfectly good as the end whereto it levels.

Problem 7: Why Hath the Common Opinion Afforded Women Souls?

It is agreed that we have not so much from them as any part of either of our mortal souls of sense or growth; and we deny souls to others equal to them in all but speech, for which they are beholding only to their bodily instruments, for perchance an ape's heart or a goat's or a fox's or a serpent's would speak just so if it were in the breast, and could move the tongue and jaws. Have they so many advantages and means to hurt us (for even their loving destroys us) that we dare not displease them, but give them what they will, and so, when some call them angels, some goddesses, and the Peputian heretics made them bishops, we descend so much with the stream to allow them souls? Or do we somewhat, in this dignifying them, flatter princes and great personages that are so much governed by them? Or do we, in that easiness and prodigality wherein we daily lose our own souls, allow souls to we care not whom, and so labour to persuade ourselves that since a woman hath a soul, a soul is no great matter? Or do we but lend them souls, and that for use, since they, for our sakes, give their souls again, and their bodies to boot? Or perchance because the Devil, who doth most mischief, is all soul, for conveniency and proportion, because they would come near him, we allow them some soul. And so as the Romans naturalized some provinces in revenge, and made them Romans only for the burden of the commonwealth, so we have given women souls only to make them capable of damnation.

Problem 8: Why Are the Fairest Falsest?

I mean not of false alchemy beauty, for then the question should be inverted, why are the falsest fairest? It is not only because they are much solicited and sought for. So is gold, yet it is not so coming. And this suit to them should teach them their value and make them more reserved. Nor is it because delicatest blood hath best spirits, for what is that to the flesh? Perchance such constitutions have the best wits, and there is no other proportionable subject for women's wits but deceit. Doth the mind so follow the temper of the body that because these complexions are aptest to change, the mind is therefore so too? Or as bells of the purest metal retain the tinkling and sound longest, so the memory of the last pleasure lasts longest in these, and disposes them to the next? But sure it is not in the complexion, for those that do but think themselves fair are presently inclined to this multiplicity of loves, which being but fair in conceit are false indeed. And so perchance when they are born to this beauty, or have made it, or have dreamt it, they easily believe all addresses and applications of every man, out of a sense of their own worthiness, to be directed to them, which others less worthy in their own thoughts apprehend not or discredit. But I think the true reason is that being like gold in many properties (as that all snatch at them, that all corruption is by them, that the worst possess them, that they care not how deep we dig for them, and that by the law of nature *occupanti conceditur*), they would be also like in this, that as gold to make itself of use admits allay, so they, that they may be tractable and malleable and current, have for their allay falsehood.

Paradox 10: That it is Possible to Find Some Virtue in Some Women

I am not of that seared impudency that I dare defend women, or pronounce them good. Yet when we see physicians allow some virtue in every poison, alas, why should we except women? Since certainly they are good for physic – at least, so as wine is good for a fever. And though they be the occasioners of most sins, they are also the punishers and revengers of the same sins. For I have seldom seen one which consumes his substance or body upon them escape diseases or beggary. And this is their justice. And if *suum cuique dare* be the fulfilling of all civil justice, they are most just: for they deny that which is theirs to no man.

Tanquam non liceat, nulla puella negat

And who may doubt of great wisdom in them, that doth but observe with how much labour and cunning our justices and other dispensers of the laws study to embrace them; and how zealously our preachers dehort men from them, only by urging their subtleties and policies and wisdom which are in them, yea, in the worst and most prostitute sort of them. Or who can deny them a good measure of fortitude, if he consider how many valiant men they have overthrown, and, being themselves overthrown, how much and how patiently they bear? And though they be all most intemperate, I care not; for I undertook to furnish them with some virtue, not all. Necessity, which makes even bad things good, prevails also for them; and we must say of them, as of some sharp punishing laws; if men were free from infirmities, they were needless; but they are both good scourges for bad men. These or none must serve for reasons; and it is my great happiness that examples prove not rules. For to confirm this opinion the world yields not one example.

IGNATIUS
HIS CONCLAVE

In the twinkling of an eye, I saw all the rooms in Hell open to my sight. And by the benefit of certain spectacles (I know not of what making, but, I think, of the same by which Gregory the Great and Beda did discern so distinctly the souls of their friends when they were discharged from their bodies, and sometimes the souls of such men as they knew not by sight, and of some that were never in the world, and yet they could distinguish them flying into Heaven or conversing with living men) I saw all the channels in the bowels of the earth; and all the inhabitants of all nations and of all ages were suddenly made familiar to me ...

Proceeding therefore to more inward places, I saw a secret place, where there were not many, beside Lucifer himself; to which only they had title which had so attempted any innovation in this life that they gave an affront to all antiquity, and induced doubts and anxieties and scruples, and, after a liberty of believing what they would, at length established opinions directly contrary to all established before ...

Now to this place not only such endeavour to come as have innovated in matters directly concerning the soul, but also they which have done so either in the arts, or in conversation, or in anything which exerciseth the faculties of the soul, and may so provoke to quarrelsome and brawling controversies. For so the truth be lost, it is no matter how. But the gates are seldom opened, nor scarce oftener than once in an age. But my destiny favoured me so much that I was present then, and saw all the pretenders, and all that affected an entrance, and Lucifer himself, who then came out into the outward chamber, to hear them plead their own causes.

As soon as the door creaked, I spied a certain mathematician, which till then had been busied to find, to deride, to detrude Ptolemy, and now with an erect countenance and settled pace came to the gates, and with his hands and feet (scarce respecting Lucifer himself) beat the doors, and cried: 'Are these shut against me, to whom all the Heavens were ever open; who was a soul to the Earth, and gave it motion?'

By this I knew it was Copernicus. For though I had never heard ill of his life, and therefore might wonder to find him there, yet when I remembered that the Papists have extended the name and the punishment of heresy almost to everything, and that as yet I used Gregory's and Bede's spectacles, by which one saw Origen, who deserved so well of the Christian church, burning in Hell, I doubted no longer, but assured myself that it was Copernicus which I saw.

To whom Lucifer said: 'Who are you? For though even by this boldness you seem worthy to enter, and have attempted a new faction even in Hell, yet you must first satisfy those which stand about you, and which expect the same fortune as you do.'

'Except, O Lucifer,' answered Copernicus, 'I thought thee of the race of the star Lucifer, with which I am so well acquainted, I should not vouchsafe thee this discourse. I am he which, pitying thee who wert thrust into the centre of the world, raised both thee and thy prison, the earth, up into the heavens; so as by my means God doth not enjoy his revenge upon thee. The sun, which was an officious spy, and a betrayer of faults, and so thine enemy, I have appointed to go into the lowest part of the world. Shall these gates be open to such as have innovated in small matters? And shall they be shut against me, who have turned the whole frame of the world, and am thereby almost a new Creator?'

More than this he spoke not. Lucifer stuck in a meditation. For what should he do? It seemed unjust to deny entry to him which had deserved so well, and dangerous to grant it to one of so great ambitions and undertakings: nor did he think that he himself had attempted greater matters before his fall. Something he had which he might have conveniently opposed, but he was loath to utter it, lest he should confess his fear.

But Ignatius Loyola, which was got near his chair, a subtle fellow, and so indued with the devil that he was able to tempt, and not only that but (as they say) even to possess the devil, apprehended this perplexity in Lucifer. And making himself sure of his own entrance, and knowing well that many thousands of his family aspired to that place, he opposed himself against all others. He was content they should be damned, but not that they should govern. And though when he died he was utterly ignorant in all great learning, and knew not so much as Ptolemy's or Copernicus's name, but might have been persuaded that the words 'Almagest', 'zenith' and 'nadir' were saints' names, and fit to be put into the Litany, and *Ora pro nobis* joined to them, yet after he had spent some time in Hell he had learnt somewhat of his Jesuits, which daily came thither. And whilst he stayed at the threshold of Hell, that is, from the time when he delivered himself over to the Pope's will, he took a little taste of learning.

Thus furnished, thus he undertakes Copernicus: 'Do you think to win our Lucifer to your part by allowing him the honour of being of the race of that star, who was not only made before all the stars, but being glutted with the glory of shining there, transferred his dwelling and colonies unto this monarchy, and thereby gave our Order a noble example to spy, to invade, and to possess foreign kingdoms? . . . But for you: what new thing have you invented by which our Lucifer gets anything? What cares he whether the earth travel or stand still? Hath your raising up of the earth into heaven brought men to that confidence that they build new towers or threaten God again? Or do they, out of this motion of the earth, conclude that there is no Hell, or deny the punishment of sin? Do not men believe? Do they not live just as they did before? Besides, this detracts from the dignity of your learning, and derogates from your right and title of coming to this place, that those opinions of yours may very well be true . . . Let therefore this little mathematician, dread Emperor, withdraw himself to his own company . . .'

Lucifer signified his assent: and Copernicus, without muttering a word, was as quiet as he thinks the sun.

SERMONS, ESSAYS
AND DEVOTIONS

Easter Monday 1622

The first book of the Bible, is a Revelation, and so is the last, in the order as they stand, a Revelation too. To declare a production of all things out of nothing, (which is Moses his work;) that when I do not know, and care not whether I know or no, what so contemptible a creature as an ant is made of, but yet would fain know what so vast, and so considerable a thing as an elephant is made of; I care not for a mustard seed, but I would fain know what a cedar is made of; I can leave out the consideration of the whole earth, but would be glad to know what the heavens, and the glorious bodies in the heavens, sun, moon and stars are made of; I shall have but one answer from Moses for all, that all my elephants, and cedars, and the heavens that I consider, were made of nothing; that a cloud is as nobly born, as the sun in the heavens; and a beggar, as nobly, as the King upon earth; if we consider the great-grandfather of them all, to be nothing: to produce light of darkness thus, is a Revelation, a manifestation of that, which, till then, was not: this Moses does. St John's is a Revelation too: a manifestation of that state, which shall be, and be for ever, after all those which were produced of nothing, shall be returned and resolved to nothing again; the glorious state of the everlasting Jerusalem, the Kingdom of Heaven ...

The drowning of the first world, and the repairing that again; the burning of this world, and establishing another in heaven, do not so much strain a man's reason, as the creation, a creation of all out of nothing. For, for the repairing of the world after the flood, compared to the creation, it was eight to nothing; eight persons to begin a world upon, then; but in the creation, none. And for the glory which we receive in the next world, it is (in some sort) as the stamping of a print upon a coin; the metal is there already, a body and a soul to receive glory: but at the creation, there was no soul to receive glory, no body to receive a soul, no stuff, no matter, to make a body of. The less any thing is, the less we know it: how invisible, how inintelligible a thing then, is this nothing! We say in the School, *Deus cognoscibilior Angelis*, We have better means to know the nature of God, than of angels, because God hath appeared and manifested himself more in actions, than angels have done: we know what they are, by knowing what they have done; and it is very little that is related to us what angels have done: what then is there that can bring this Nothing to our understanding? What hath that done? A Leviathan, a whale, from a grain of spawn; an oak from a buried acorn, is a great; but a great world from nothing, is a strange improvement. We wonder to see a man rise from nothing to a great estate; but that nothing is nothing in comparison; but absolutely nothing, merely nothing, is more incomprehensible than any thing, than all things together. It is a state (if a man may call it a state) that the Devil himself in the midst of his torments, cannot wish. No man can, the Devil himself cannot, advisedly, deliberately, wish himself to be nothing. It is truly and safely said in the School, That whatsoever can be the subject of a wish, if I can desire it, wish it, it must necessarily be better (at least in my opinion) than that which I have; and whatsoever is better, is not nothing; without doubt it must necessarily produce more thankfulness in me, towards God, that I am a Christian; but certainly more wonder that I am a creature: it is vehemently spoken, but yet needs no excuse, which Justin Martyr says, *Ne ipsi quidem Domino fidem haberem, &c.* I should scarce believe God himself, if he should tell me, that any but himself created this world of nothing; so infallible, and so inseparable a work, and so distinctive a character is it of the Godhead, to produce anything from nothing; and that God did when he commanded light out of darkness . . .

Lincoln's Inn, 1618 (I)

This captivity to sin, comes so swiftly, so impetuously upon us. Consider it first in our making; In the generation of our parents, we were conceived in sin;

that is, they sinned in that action; so we were conceived in sin; in their sin. And in our selves, we were submitted to sin, in that very act of generation, because then we became in part the subject of original sin. Yet, there was no arrow shot into us then; there was no sin in that substance of which we were made; for if there had been sin in that substance, that substance might be damned, though God should never infuse a soul into it; and that cannot be said well then: God, whose goodness, and wisdom will have that substance to become a man, he creates a soul for it, or creates a soul in it, (I dispute not that) he sends a light, or he kindles a light, in that lanthorn; and here's no arrow shot neither; here's no sin in that soul, that God creates; for there God should create something that were evil; and that cannot be said: Here's no arrow shot from the body, no sin in the body alone; None from the soul, no sin in the soul alone; And yet, the union of this soul and body is so accompanied with God's malediction for our first transgression, that in the instant of that union of life, as certainly as that body must die, so certainly the whole man must be guilty of original sin. No man can tell me out of what quiver, yet here is an arrow comes so swiftly, as that in the very first minute of our life, in our quickening in our mother's womb, we become guilty of Adam's sin done 6000 years before, and subject to all those arrows, hunger, labour, grief, sickness, and death, which have been shot after it. This is the fearful swiftness of this arrow, that God himself cannot get before it. In the first minute that my soul is infused, the image of God is imprinted in my soul; so forward is God in my behalf, and so early does he visit me. But yet original sin is there, as soon as that image of God is there. My soul is capable of God as soon as it is capable of sin; and though sin do not get the start of God, God does not get the start of sin neither. Powers, that dwell so far asunder, as Heaven, and Hell, God and the Devil, meet in an instant in my soul, in the minute of my quickening, and the image of God and the Image of Adam, original sin, enter into me at once, in one, and the same act. So swift is this arrow, original sin, from which, all arrows of subsequent temptations, are shot, as that God, who comes to my first minute of life, cannot come before death.

Lincoln's Inn, 1618 (II)

But except we do come to say, Our sins are our own, God will never cut up that root in us, God will never blot out the memory in himself, of those sins. Nothing can make them none of ours, but the avowing of them, the confessing of them to be ours. Only in this way, I am a holy liar, and in this the God of truth will reward my lie; for, if I say my sins are mine own, they are none of mine, but, by that confessing and appropriating of

211

those sins to my self, they are made the sins of him, who hath suffered enough for all, my blessed Lord and Saviour, Christ Jesus. Therefore that servant of God, St Augustine confesses those sins, which he never did, to be his sins, and to have been forgiven him: *Peccata mihi dimissa fateor, et quæ mea sponte feci, et quæ te duce non feci*; Those sins which I have done, and those, which, but for thy grace, I should have done, are all, my sins. Alas, I may die here, and die under an everlasting condemnation of fornication with that woman, that lives, and dies a virgin, and be damned for a murderer of that man, that outlives me, and for a robbery, and oppression, where no man is damnified, nor any penny lost. The sin that I have done, the sin that I would have done, is my sin . . .

From *Essays in Divinity*

. . . Of all the ways in which God hath expressed himself towards us, we have made no word which doth less signify what we mean than 'power': for power, which is but an ability to do, ever relates to some future thing, and God is ever present, simple, and pure act. But we think we have done much and gone far when we have made up the word 'omnipotence' – which is both ways improper; for it is much too short, because omnipotence supposes and confesses a matter and subject to work upon, and yet God was the same when there was nothing. And then it over-reaches and goes downward beyond God: for God hath not, or is not, such an omnipotence as can do all things. For though squeamish and tenderer men think it more mannerly to say *This thing cannot be done* than *God cannot do this thing*, yet it is all one. And if that be an omnipotence which is limited with the nature of the worker, or with the congruity of the subject, other things may encroach upon the word *omnipotent*; that is, they can do all things which are not against their nature or the nature of the matter upon which they work. Beza therefore might well enough say that God could not make a body without place; and Prateolus might truly enough infer upon that, that the Bezanites (as he calls them) deny omnipotence in God. For both are true. And therefore I doubt not that it hath some mystery that the word 'omnipotence' is not found in all the Bible, nor 'omnipotent' in the New Testament. And where it is in the Old, it would rather be interpreted 'all-sufficient' than 'almighty' – between which there is much difference. God is so all-sufficient that he is sufficient for all, and sufficient to all. He is enough, and we are in him able enough to take and apply. We fetch part of our wealth, which is our faith, expressly from his treasury; and for our good works, we bring the metal to his mint (or that mint comes to us) and there the character of baptism and the impression of his grace makes them current and somewhat worth, even towards him. God is all-efficient: that is, hath created the beginning, ordained the way, foreseen the end of everything; and nothing else is any kind of cause thereof. Yet since this word 'efficient' is now grown to signify infallibility in God, it reaches not home to that which we mean of God; since man is efficient cause of his own destruction. God is also *all-conficient*, that is, concurs with the nature of everything; for indeed the nature of everything is that which he works in it. And as he redeemed not man as he was God (though the mercy and purpose and acceptation were only of God) but as God and man, so in our repentances and reconciliations, though the first grace proceed only from God, yet we concur so, as there is an union of two hypostases, grace and nature. Which (as the incarnation of our blessed Saviour himself was) is conceived in us of the Holy Ghost, without father, but fed and produced by us, that is, by our will, first enabled and illumined. For neither God nor man determine man's will (for that must either imply a necessiting thereof from God, or else Pelagianism) but they condetermine it. And thus God is truly all-conficient, that is, concurrent in all; and yet we may not dare to say that he hath any part in sin. So God is also all-perficient: that is, all and all parts of every work are his entirely; and lest any might seem to escape him and be attributed to nature or to art, all things were in him at once before he made nature, or she art. All things which we do today were done by us in him before we were made. And now (when they are produced in time, as they were foreseen in eternity) his exciting grace provokes every particular good work, and his assisting grace perfects it. And yet we may not say but that God begins many things which we frustrate, and calls when we come not. So that as yet our understanding hath found no word which is well proportioned to that which we mean by 'power of God'...

... All ordinary significations of justice will conveniently be reduced to these two: innocence, which in the Scriptures is everywhere called righteousness; or else satisfaction for transgressions, which, though Christ have paid aforehand for us all, and so we are rather pardoned than put to satisfaction, yet we are bound at God's tribunal to plead our pardon and to pay the fees of contrition and penance. For since our justification now consists not in a pacification of God (for then nothing but that which is infinite could have any proportion) but in the application of the merits of Christ to us, our contrition (which is a compassion with Christ, and so an incorporating of ourselves into his merit) hath *aliqualem proportionem* to God's justice; and the passion of Christ had not *aequalem*, but that God's acceptation (which also dignifies our contrition, though not to that height) advanced it to that worthiness. To enquire further the way and manner by which God makes a few do acceptable works, or how out of a corrupt lump he selects and purifies a few, is but a stumbling block and a temptation. Who asks a charitable man that gives him an alms, where he got it, or why he gave it? Will any favourite, whom his Prince, only for his appliableness to him, or some half-virtue, or his own glory, burdens with honours and fortunes every day, and destines to future offices and dignities, dispute or expostulate with his Prince why he rather chose not another, how he will restore his coffers, how he will quench his people's murmurings by whom this liberality is fed, or his nobility, with whom he equals new men; and will not rather repose himself gratefully in the wisdom, greatness, and bounty of his master? Will a languishing desperate patient, that hath scarce time enough to swallow the potion, examine the physician, how he procured those ingredients, how that soil nourished them, which humour they affect in the body, whether they work by excess of quality, or specifically; whether he have prepared them by correcting, or else by withdrawing their malignity; and for such unnecessary scruples neglect his health? Alas, our time is little enough for prayer, and praise, and society; which is, for our mutual duties. Moral divinity becomes us all; but natural divinity, and metaphysic divinity, almost all may spare . . .

Divers men may walk by the sea side, and the same beams of the sun giving light to them all, one gathereth by the benefit of that light pebbles, or speckled shells, for curious vanity, and another gathers precious pearl, or medicinal amber, by the same light. So the common light of reason illumines us all; but one employs this light upon the searching of impertinent vanities, another by a better use of the same light, finds out the mysteries of religion; and when he hath found them, loves them, not for the light's sake, but for the natural and true worth of the thing itself. Some men by the benefit of this light of reason, have found out things profitable and useful to the whole world; As in particular, printing, by which the learning of the whole world is communicable to one another, and our minds and our inventions, our wits and compositions may trade and have commerce together, and we may participate of one another's understandings, as well as of our clothes, and wines, and oils, and other merchandize: So by the benefit of this light of reason, they have found out artillery, by which wars come to quicker ends than heretofore, and the great expense of blood is avoided: for the numbers of men slain now, since the invention of artillery, are much less than before, when the sword was the executioner. Others, by the benefit of this light have searched and found the secret corners of gain and profit, wheresoever they lie. They have found wherein the weakness of another man consisteth, and made their profit of that, by circumventing him in a bargain: They have found his riotous, and wasteful inclination, and they have fed and fomented that disorder, and kept open that leak, to their advantage, and the other's ruin. They have found where was the easiest, and most accessible way, to solicit the chastity of a woman, whether discourse, music, or presents, and according to that discovery, they have pursued hers, and their own eternal destruction. By the benefit of this light, men see through the darkest, and most impervious places, that are, that is, Courts of Princes, and the greatest Officers in Courts; and can submit themselves to second, and to advance the humours of men in great place, and so make their profit of the weaknesses which they have discovered in these great men. All the ways, both of wisdom, and of craft lie open to this light, this light of natural reason: But when they have gone all these ways by the benefit of this light, they have got no further, than to have walked by a tempestuous sea, and to have gathered pebbles, and speckled cockle shells. Their light seems to be great out of the same reason, that a torch in a misty night, seemeth greater than in a clear, because it hath kindled and inflamed much thick and gross air round about it. So the light and wisdom of worldly men, seemeth great, because he hath kindled an admiration, or an applause in airy flatterers, not because it is so indeed . . .

2 February 1623

The Church is the house of prayer, so, as that upon occasion, preaching may be left out, but never a house of preaching, so, as that prayer may be left out. And for the debt of prayer, God will not be paid, with money of our own coining, (with sudden, extemporal, inconsiderate prayer) but with current money, that bears the King's image, and inscription; The Church of God, by his ordinance, hath set his stamp, upon a liturgy and service, for his house. *Audit Deus in corde cogitantis, quod nec ipse audit, qui cogitat*, says St Bernard: God hears the very first motions of a man's heart, which, that man, till he proceed to a farther consideration, doth not hear, not feel, not deprehend in himself.

That soul, that is accustomed to direct herself to God, upon every occasion, that, as a flower at sun-rising, conceives a sense of God, in every beam of his, and spreads and dilates itself towards him, in a thankfulness, in every small blessing that he sheds upon her; that soul, that as a flower at the sun's declining, contracts and gathers in, and shuts up herself, as though she had received a blow, whensoever she hears her Saviour wounded by an oath, or blasphemy, or execration; that soul, who, whatsoever string be strucken in her, base or treble, her high or her low estate, is ever tuned toward God, that soul prays sometimes when it does not know that it prays. I hear that man name God, and ask him what said you, and perchance he cannot tell; but I remember, that he casts forth some of those *ejaculationes animæ*, (as St Augustine calls them) some of those darts of a devout soul, which, though they have not particular deliberations, and be not formal prayers, yet they are the *indicia*, pregnant evidences and blessed fruits of a religious custom; much more is it true, which St Bernard says there, of them, *Deus audit*, God hears that voice of the heart, which the heart itself hears not, that is, at first considers not. Those occasional and transitory prayers, and those fixed and stationary prayers, for which, many times, we bind ourselves to private prayer at such a time, are payments of this debt, in such pieces, and in such sums, as God, no doubt, accepts at our hands. But yet the solemn days of payment, are the sabbaths of the Lord, and the place of this payment, is the house of the Lord, where, as Tertullian expresses it, *Agmine facto*, we muster our forces together, and besiege God; that is, not taking up every tattered fellow, every sudden rag or fragment of speech, that rises from our tongue, or our affections, but mustering up those words, which the Church hath levied for that service, in the confessions, and absolutions, and collects, and litanies of the Church, we pay this debt, and we receive our acquittance.

Heidelberg, 16 June 1619

As he that travels weary, and late towards a great city, is glad when he comes to a place of execution, because he knows that is near the town; so when thou comest to the gate of death, be glad of that, for it is but one step from that to thy Jerusalem. Christ hath brought us in some nearness to salvation, as he is *vere Salvator mundi* in that we know, that this is indeed the Christ, the Saviour of the world: and he hath brought it nearer than that, as he is *Salvator corporis sui*, in that we know, That Christ is the head of the Church, and the Saviour of that body: And nearer than that, as he is *Salvator tuus sanctus*, In that we know, He is the Lord our God, the holy One of Israel, our Saviour: But nearest of all, in the *Ecce Salvator tuus venit*, Behold thy Salvation cometh. It is not only promised in the prophets, nor only writ in the gospel, nor only sealed in the sacraments, nor only prepared in the visitations of the Holy Ghost, but *Ecce*, behold it, now, when thou canst behold nothing else: The sun is setting to thee, and that for ever; thy houses and furnitures, thy gardens and orchards, thy titles and offices, thy wife and children are departing from thee, and that for ever; a cloud of faintness is come over thine eyes, and a cloud of sorrow over all theirs; when his hand that loves thee best hangs tremblingly over thee to close thine eyes, *Ecce Salvator tuus venit,* behold then a new light, thy Saviour's hand shall open thine eyes, and in his light thou shalt see light; and thus shalt see, that though in the eyes of men thou lie upon that bed, as a statue on a tomb, yet in the eyes of God, thou standest as a colossus, one foot in one, another in another land; one foot in the grave, but the other in heaven; one hand in the womb of the earth, and the other in Abraham's bosom.

From DEVOTIONS UPON EMERGENT
OCCASIONS

XVI ET PROPERARE MEUM CLAMANT, E TURRE
PROPINQUA, OBSTREPERÆ CAMPANÆ ALIORUM IN
FUNERE, FUNUS

XVI *Meditation*

We have a convenient author, who writ a discourse of
bells when he was prisoner in Turkey. How would he
have enlarged himself if he had been my fellow-prisoner
in this sick bed, so near to that steeple which never
ceases, no more than the harmony of the spheres, but is
more heard. When the Turks took Constantinople, they
melted the bells into ordnance; I have heard both bells
and ordnance, but never been so much affected with
those as with these bells. I have lain near a steeple in
which there are said to be more than thirty bells, and
near another, where there is one so big, as that the
clapper is said to weigh more than six hundred pound,
yet never so affected as here. Here the bells can scarce
solemnize the funeral of any person, but that I knew
him, or knew that he was my neighbour: we dwelt in
houses near to one another before, but now he is gone
into that house into which I must follow him. There is a
way of correcting the children of great persons, that
other children are corrected in their behalf, and in their
names, and this works upon them who indeed had more

deserved it. And when these bells tell me, that now one, and now another is buried, must not I acknowledge that they have the correction due to me, and paid the debt that I owe? There is a story of a bell in a monastery which, when any of the house was sick to death, rung always voluntarily, and they knew the inevitableness of the danger by that. It rung once when no man was sick, but the next day one of the house fell from the steeple and died, and the bell held the reputation of a prophet still. If these bells that warn to a funeral now, were appropriated to none, may not I, by the hour of the funeral, supply? How many men that stand at an execution, if they would ask, For what dies that man? should hear their own faults condemned, and see themselves executed by attorney? We scarce hear of any man preferred, but we think of ourselves, that we might very well have been that man; why might not I have been that man that is carried to his grave now? Could I fit myself to stand or sit in any man's place, and not to lie in any man's grave? I may lack much of the good parts of the meanest, but I lack nothing of the mortality of the weakest; they may have acquired better abilities than I, but I was born to as many infirmities as they. To be an incumbent by lying down in a grave, to be a doctor by teaching mortification by example, by dying, though I may have seniors, others may be older than I, yet I have proceeded apace in a good university, and gone a great way in a little time, by the furtherance of a vehement fever; and whomsoever these bells bring to the ground to-day, if he and I had been compared yesterday, perchance I should have been thought likelier to come to this preferment then than he. God hath kept the power of death in his own hands, lest any man should bribe death. If man knew the gain of death, the ease of death, he would solicit, he would provoke death to assist him by any hand which he might use. But as when men see many of their own professions preferred, it ministers a hope that that may light upon them; so when these hourly bells tell me of so many funerals of men like me, it presents, if not a desire that it may, yet a comfort whensoever mine shall come ...

XVII NUNC LENTO SONITU DICUNT, MORIERIS

XVII *Meditation*

Perchance he for whom this bell tolls may be so ill, as that he knows not it tolls for him; and perchance I may think myself so much better than I am, as that they who are about me, and see my state, may have caused it to toll for me, and I know not that. The church is Catholic, universal, so are all her actions; all that she does belongs to all. When she baptizes a child, that action concerns me; for that child is thereby connected to that head which is my head too, and ingrafted into that body whereof I am a member. And when she buries a man, that action concerns me: all mankind is of one author, and is one volume; when one man dies, one chapter is not torn out of the book, but translated into a better language; and every chapter must be so translated; God employs several translators; some pieces are translated by age, some by sickness, some by war, some by justice; but God's hand is in every translation, and his hand shall bind up all our scattered leaves again, for that library where every book shall lie open to one another. As therefore the bell that rings to a sermon calls not upon the preacher only, but upon the congregation to come, so this bell calls us all; but how much more me, who am brought so near the door by this sickness. There was a contention as far as a suit (in which both piety and dignity, religion and estimation, were mingled), which of the religious orders should ring to prayers first in the morning; and it was determined, that they should ring first that rose earliest. If we understand aright the dignity of this bell that tolls for our evening prayer, we would be glad to make it ours by rising early, in that application, that it might be ours as well as his, whose indeed it is. The bell doth toll for him that thinks it doth; and though it intermit again, yet from that minute that that occasion wrought upon him, he is united to God. Who casts not up his eye to the sun when it rises? But who takes off his eye from a comet when that breaks out? Who bends not his ear to any bell which upon any occasion rings? But who can remove it from that bell which is passing a piece of himself out of this world? No man is an island, entire of itself; every man is a piece of the continent, a part of the main. If a clod be washed away by the sea, Europe is the less, as well as if a promontory were, as well as if a manor of thy friend's or of thine own were: any man's death diminishes me, because I am involved in mankind, and therefore never send to know for whom the bell tolls; it tolls for thee. Neither can we call this a begging of misery, or a borrowing of misery, as though we were not miserable enough of ourselves, but must fetch in more from the next house, in taking upon us the misery of our neighbours. Truly it were an excusable covetousness if we did, for affliction is a treasure, and scarce any man hath enough of it. No man hath affliction enough that is not matured and ripened by it, and made fit for God by that affliction. If a man carry treasure in bullion, or in a wedge of gold, and have none coined into current monies, his treasure will not defray him as he travels. Tribulation is treasure in the nature of it, but it is not current money in the use of it, except we get nearer and nearer our home, heaven, by it. Another man may be sick too, and sick to death, and this affliction may lie in his bowels, as gold in a mine, and be of no use to him; but this bell, that tells me of his affliction, digs out and applies that gold to me, if by this consideration of another's danger I take mine own into contemplation, and so secure myself, by making my course to my God, who is our only security.

XVIII At inde mortuus es, sonitu celeri, pulsuque agitato

XVIII *Meditation*

The bell rings out, the pulse thereof is changed; the tolling was a faint and intermitting pulse, upon one side; this stronger, and argues more and better life. His soul is gone out; and as a man who had a lease of one thousand years after the expiration of a short one, or an inheritance after the life of a man in a consumption, he is now entered into the possession of his better estate. His soul is gone, whither? Who saw it come in, or who saw it go out? Nobody; yet everybody is sure he had one, and hath none. If I will ask mere philosophers what the soul is, I shall find amongst them that will tell me, it is nothing but the temperament and harmony, and just and equal composition of the elements in the body, which produces all those faculties which we ascribe to the soul; and so in itself is nothing, no separable substance that overlives the body. They see the soul is nothing else in other creatures, and they affect an impious humility to think as low of man. But if my soul were no more than the soul of a beast, I could not think so; that soul that can reflect upon itself, consider itself, is more than so. If I will ask, not mere philosophers, but mixed men, philosophical divines, how the soul, being a separate substance, enters into man, I shall find some that will tell me, that it is by generation and procreation from parents, because they think it hard to charge the soul with the guiltiness of original sin if the soul were infused into a body, in which it must necessary grow foul, and contract original sin whether it will or no; and I shall find some that will tell me, that it is by immediate infusion from God, because they think it hard to maintain an immortality in such a soul, as should be begotten and derived with the body from mortal parents. If I will ask, not a few men, but almost whole bodies, whole churches, what becomes of the souls of the righteous at the departing thereof from the body, I shall be told by some, that they attend an expiation, a purification in a place of torment; by some, that they attend the fruition of the sight of God in a place of rest, but yet but of expectation; by some, that they pass to an immediate possession of the presence of God. St Augustine studied the nature of the soul, as much as anything, but the salvation of the soul; and he sent an express messenger to St Jerome, to consult of some things concerning the soul; but he satisfies himself with this: 'Let the departure of my soul to salvation be evident to my faith, and I care the less how dark the entrance of my soul into my body be to my reason'. It is the going out, more than the coming in, that concerns us. This soul, this bell tells me, is gone out; whither? Who shall tell me that? I know not who it is, much less what he was. The condition of the man, and the course of his life, which should tell me whither he is gone, I know not. I was not there in his sickness, nor at his death; I saw not his way nor his end, nor can ask them who did, thereby to conclude or argue whither he is gone. But yet I have one nearer me than all these, mine own charity; I ask that, and that tells me he is gone to everlasting rest, and joy, and glory. I owe him a good opinion; it is but thankful charity in me, because I received benefit and instruction from him when his bell tolled; and I, being made the fitter to pray by that disposition, wherein I was assisted by his occasion, did pray for him; and I pray not without faith; So I do charitably, so I do faithfully believe, that that soul is gone to everlasting rest, and joy, and glory. But for the body, how poor a wretched thing is that? We cannot express it so fast, as it grows worse and worse. That body, which scarce three minutes since was such a house as that that soul, which made but one step from thence to heaven, was scarce thoroughly content to leave that for heaven; that body hath lost the name of a dwelling-house, because none dwells in it, and is making haste to lose the name of a body, and dissolve to putrefaction. Who would not be affected to see a clear and sweet river in the morning, grow a kennel of muddy land-water by noon, and condemned to the saltness of the sea by night? And how lame a picture, how faint a representation is that, of the precipitation of man's body to dissolution? Now all the parts built up, and knit by a lovely soul, now but a statue of clay, and now these limbs melted off, as if that clay were but snow; and now the whole house is but a handful of sand, so much dust, and but a peck of rubbish, so much bone. If he who, as this bell tells me, is gone now, were some excellent artificer, who comes to him for a cloak or for a garment now? Or for counsel, if he were a lawyer? If a magistrate, for justice? Man, before he hath his immortal soul, hath a soul of sense, and a soul of vegetation before that: this immortal soul did not forbid other souls to be in us before, but when this soul departs, it carries all with it; no more vegetation, no more sense. Such a mother-in-law is the earth, in respect of our natural mother; in her womb we grew, and when she was delivered of us, we were planted in some place, in some calling in the world; in the womb of the earth we diminish, and when she is delivered of us, our grave opened for another; we are not transplanted, but transported, our dust blown away with profane dust, with every wind ...

...That which we call life is but *hebdomada mortium*, a week of death, seven days, seven periods of our life spent in dying, a dying seven times over; and there is an end. Our birth dies in infancy, and our infancy dies in youth, and youth and the rest die in age, and age also dies and determines all. Nor do all these, youth out of infancy, or age out of youth, arise so, as a phoenix out of the ashes of another phoenix formerly dead, but as a wasp or a serpent out of a carrion, or as a snake out of dung. Our youth is worse than our infancy, and our age worse than our youth. Our youth is hungry and thirsty after those sins which our infancy knew not; and our age is sorry and angry, that it cannot pursue those sins which our youth did. And besides, all the way, so many deaths, that is, so many deadly calamities accompany every condition and every period of this life, as that death itself would be an ease to them that suffer them. Upon this sense doth Job wish that God had not given him an issue from the first death, from the womb, *Wherefore hast thou brought me forth out of the womb? Oh that I had given up the ghost, and no eye had seen me! I should have been as though I had not been.* And not only the impatient Israelites in their murmuring (*would to God we had died by the hand of the Lord in the land of Egypt*), but Elijah himself, when he fled from Jezebel, and went for his life, as the text says, under the juniper tree, requested that he might die, and said, *It is enough now, O Lord, take away my life.* So Jonah justifies his impatience, nay, his anger, towards God himself: *Now, O Lord, take, I beseech thee, my life from me, for it is better for me to die than to live.* And when God asked him, *Dost thou well to be angry for this?* and after (about the gourd) *dost thou well to be angry for that?* he replies, *I do well to be angry, even unto death.* How much worse a death than death is this life, which so good men would so often change for death! But if my case be as Saint Paul's case, *quotidiè morior*, that I die daily, that something heavier than death fall upon me every day; if my case be David's case, *tota die mortificamur; all the day long we are killed*, that not only every day, but every hour of the day, something heavier than death fall upon me; though that be true of me, *Conceptus in peccatis, I was shapen in iniquity, and in sin did my mother conceive me* (there I died one death); though that be true of me, *Natus filius iræ*, I was born not only the child of sin, but the child of wrath, of the wrath of God for sin, which is a heavier death: yet *Domini Domini sunt exitus mortis, with God the Lord are the issues of death*; and after a Job, and a Joseph, and a Jeremiah, and a Daniel, I cannot doubt of a deliverance. And if no other deliverance conduce more to his glory and my good, yet he hath the keys of death, and he can let me out at that door, that is, deliver me from the manifold deaths of this world, the *omni die*, and the *tota die*, the every day's death and every hour's death, by that one death, the final dissolution of body and soul, the end of all. But then is that the end of all? Is that dissolution of body and soul the last death that the body shall suffer (for of spiritual death we speak not now)? It is not. Though this be *exitus à morte*: it is *introitus in mortem*; though it be an issue from manifold deaths of this world, yet it is an entrance into the death of corruption and putrefaction, and vermiculation, and incineration, and dispersion in and from the grave, in which every dead man dies over again. It was a prerogative peculiar to Christ, not to die this death, not to see corruption. What gave him this privilege? Not Joseph's great proportion of gums and spices, that might have preserved his body from corruption and incineration longer than he needed it, longer than three days, but it would not have done it for ever. What preserved him then? Did his exemption and freedom from original sin preserve him from this corruption and incineration? 'Tis true that original sin hath induced this corruption and incineration upon us; if we had not sinned in Adam, *mortality had not put on immortality* (as the apostle speaks), nor *corruption had not put on incorruption*, but we had had our transmigration from this to the other world without any mortality, any corruption at all. But yet since Christ took sin upon him, so far as made him mortal, he had it so far too as might have made him see this corruption and incineration, though he had no original sin in himself. What preserved him then? Did the hypostatical union of both natures, God and man, preserve him from this corruption and incineration? 'Tis true that this was a most powerful embalming, to be embalmed with the divine nature itself, to be embalmed with eternity, was able to preserve him from corruption and incineration for ever. And he was embalmed so, embalmed with the divine nature itself, even in his body as well as in his soul; for the Godhead, the divine nature, did not depart, but remained still united to his dead body in the grave. But yet for all this powerful embalming, his hypostatical union of both natures, we see Christ did die; and for all this union which made him God and man, he became no man (for the union of the body and soul makes the man, and he whose soul and body are separated by death, as long as that state lasts, is properly no man). And therefore as in him the dissolution of body and soul was no dissolution of the hypostatical union, so is there nothing that constrains us to say, that though the flesh of Christ had seen corruption and incineration in the grave, this had been any dissolution of the hypostatical union, for the divine nature, the Godhead, might have remained with all the elements and principles of Christ's body, as well as it did with the two constitutive parts of his person, his body and his soul. This incorruption then was not in Joseph's gums and spices, nor was it in Christ's innocency, and exemption from original sin, nor was it (that is, it is not necessary to say it was) in the hypostatical union. But this incorruptibleness of his flesh is most conveniently placed in that; *Non dabis, thou wilt not suffer thy Holy One to see corruption*; we look no further for causes or reasons in the mysteries of religion, but to the will and pleasure of God; Christ himself limited his inquisition in that *ita est, even so, Father, for so it seemed good in thy sight.* Christ's body did not see corruption, therefore, because God had decreed it should not. The humble soul (and only the humble soul is the religious soul) rests himself upon God's purposes, and his decrees; but then, it is upon those purposes, and decrees of God which he hath declared and manifested, not such as are conceived and imagined in ourselves, though upon some probability, some verisimilitude. So, in our present case, Peter proceeded in his sermon at Jerusalem, and so Paul in his at Antioch. They preached Christ to have been risen without seeing corruption, not only because God had decreed it, but because he had manifested that decree in his prophet. Therefore doth Saint Paul cite by special number the second Psalm for that decree; and therefore both Saint Peter and Saint Paul cite for it that place in the sixteenth Psalm; for when God declares his decree and purpose in the express words of his prophet, or when he declares it in the real execution of the decree, then he makes it ours, then he manifests it to us. And therefore, as the mysteries of our religion are not the objects of our reason, but by faith we rest on God's decree and purpose (it is so, O God, because it is thy will it should be so) so God's decrees are ever to be considered in the manifestation thereof. All manifestation is either in the word of God, or in the execution of the decree; and when these two concur and meet it is the strongest demonstration that can be: when therefore I find those marks of adoption and spiritual filiation which are delivered in the word of God to be upon me; when I find that real execution of his good purpose upon me, as that actually I do live under the obedience and under the conditions which are evidences of adoption and spiritual filiation; then, and so long as I see these marks and live so, I may safely comfort myself in a holy certitude and a modest infallibility of my adoption. Christ determines himself in that, the purpose of God; because the purpose of God was manifest to him; Saint Peter and Saint Paul determine themselves in those two ways of knowing the purpose of God, the word of God before the execution of the decree in the fulness of time. It was prophesied before, say they, and it is performed now, Christ is risen without seeing corruption. Now, this which is so singularly peculiar to him, that his flesh should not see corruption, at his second coming, his coming to judgment, shall extend to all that are then alive; their flesh shall not see corruption, because (as the apostle says, and says as a secret, as a mystery, *Behold I shew you a mystery*) *we shall not all sleep* (that is, not continue in the state of the dead in the grave), *but we shall all be changed*. In an instant, we shall have a dissolution, and in the same instant a redintegration, a recompacting of body and soul, and that shall be truly a death and truly a resurrection, but no sleeping, no corruption. But for us that die now and sleep in the state of the dead, we must all pass this posthume death, this death after death, nay, this death after burial, this dissolution after dissolution, this death of corruption and putrefaction, of vermiculation and incineration, of dissolution and dispersion in and from the grave. When those bodies that have been the children of royal parents, and the parents of royal children, must say with Job, *to corruption, thou art my father*, and *to the worm, thou art my mother and my sister*. Miserable riddle, when the same worm must be my mother, and my sister and myself. Miserable incest, when I must be married to my mother and my sister, and be both father and mother to my own mother and sister, beget and bear that worm which is all that miserable penury; when my mouth shall be filled with dust, and the *worm shall feed, and feed sweetly* upon me; when the ambitious man shall have no satisfaction, if the poorest alive tread upon him, nor the poorest receive any contentment in being made equal to princes, for they shall be equal but in dust. One dieth at his full strength, being wholly at ease and in quiet; and another dies in the *bitterness of his soul*, and never *eats with pleasure*; but *they lie down alike in the dust, and the worm covers them.* The worm covers them in Job and in Isaiah, it covers them and is spread under them, *the worm is spread under thee, and the worm covers thee.* There's the mats and the carpets that lie under, and there's the state and the canopy that hangs over the greatest of the sons of men. Even those bodies that were *the temples of the Holy Ghost* come to this dilapidation, to ruin, to rubbish, to dust; even the Israel of the Lord, and Jacob himself, hath no other specification, no other denomination, but that *vermis Jacob*, thou worm of Jacob. Truly the consideration of this posthume death, this death after burial, that after God (with whom are the issues of death) hath delivered me from the death of the womb, by bringing me into the world, and from the manifold deaths of the world, by laying me in the grave, I must die again in an incineration of this flesh, and in a dispersion of that dust; that that monarch, who spread over many nations alive, must in his dust lie in a corner of that sheet of lead, and there but so long as that lead will last; and that private and retired man, that thought himself his own for ever, and never came forth, must in his dust of the grave be published, and (such are the revolutions of the graves) be mingled in his dust with the dust of every highway and of every dunghill, and swallowed in every puddle and pond: this is the most inglorious and contemptible vilification, the most deadly and peremptory nullification of man, that we can consider. God seems to have carried the declaration of his power to a great height, when he sets the prophet Ezekiel in the valley of dry bones, and says, *Son of man, can these bones live?* as though it had been impossible, and yet they did; the Lord laid *sinews upon them, and flesh, and breathed into them, and they did live*. But in that case there were bones to be seen, something visible, of which it might be said, Can this thing live? But in this death of incineration and dispersion of dust, we see nothing that we can call that man's. If we say, can this dust live? perchance it cannot; it may be the mere dust of the earth, which never did live, nor never shall. It may be the dust of that man's worms which did live, but shall no more. It may be the dust of another man, that concerns not him of whom it is asked. This death of incineration and dispersion is, to natural reason, the most irrecoverable death of all; and yet *Domini Domini sunt exitus mortis, unto God the Lord belong the issues of death*; and by recompacting this dust into the same body, and re-animating the same body with the same soul, he shall in a blessed and glorious resurrection give me such an issue from this death as shall never pass into any other death, but establish me into a life that shall last as long as the Lord of Life himself.

From *A Sermon preached to the Earl of Carlisle, 1622*

...That then there is damnation, and why it is, and when it is, is clear enough; but what this damnation is, neither the tongue of good angels that know damnation by the contrary, by fruition of salvation, nor the tongue of bad angels who know damnation by a lamentable experience, is able to express it; A man may sail so at sea, as that he shall have laid the North Pole flat, that shall be fallen out of sight, and yet he shall not have raised the South Pole, he shall not see that; So there are things, in which a man may go beyond his reason, and yet not meet with faith neither: of such a kind are those things which concern the locality of hell, and the materiality of the torments thereof; for that hell is a certain and limited place, beginning here and ending there, and extending no farther, or that the torments of hell be material, or elementary torments, which in natural consideration can have no proportion, no affection, nor appliableness to the tormenting of a spirit, these things neither settle my reason, nor bind my faith; neither opinion, that it is, or is not so, doth command our reason so, but that probable reasons may be brought on the other side; neither opinion doth so command our faith, but that a man may be saved, though he think the contrary; for in such points, it is always lawful to think so, as we find does most advance and exalt our own devotion, and God's glory in our estimation; but when we shall have given to those words, by which hell is expressed in the Scriptures, the heaviest significations, that either the nature of those words can admit, or as they are types and representations of hell, as *fire*, and *brimstone*, and *weeping*, and *gnashing*, and *darkness*, and *the worm*, and as they are laid together in the prophet, *Tophet*, (that is, hell) *is deep and large*, (there is the capacity and content, room enough) *It is a pile of fire and much wood*, (there is the durableness of it) *and the breath of the Lord to kindle it, like a stream of brimstone*, (there is the vehemence of it:) when all is done, the hell of hells, the torment of torments is the everlasting absence of God, and the everlasting impossibility of returning to his presence; *Horrendum est*, says the apostle, *It is a fearful thing to fall into the hands of the living God*. Yet there was a case, in which David found an ease, to fall into the hands of God, to scape the hands of men: *Horrendum est*, when God's hand is bent to strike, *it is a fearful thing, to fall into the hands of the living God*; but to fall out of the hands of the living God, is a horror beyond our expression, beyond our imagination.

That God should let my soul fall out of his hand, into

a bottomless pit, and roll an unremoveable stone upon it, and leave it to that which it finds there, (and it shall find that there, which it never imagined, till it came thither) and never think more of that soul, never have more to do with it. That of that providence of God, that studies the life and preservation of every weed, and worm, and ant, and spider, and toad, and viper, there should never, never any beam flow out upon me; that that God, who looked upon me, when I was nothing, and called me when I was not, as though I had been, out of the womb and depth of darkness, will not look upon me now, when, though a miserable, and a banished, and a damned creature, yet I am his creature still, and contribute something to his glory, even in my damnation; that that God, who hath often looked upon me in my foulest uncleanness, and when I had shut out of the eye of the day, the sun, and the eye of the night, the taper, and the eyes of all the world, with curtains and windows and doors, did yet see me, and see me in mercy, by making me see that he saw me, and sometimes brought me to a present remorse, and (for that time) to a forbearing of that sin, should so turn himself from me, to his glorious saints and angels, as that no saint nor angel, nor Christ Jesus himself, should ever pray him to look towards me, never remember him, that such a soul there is; that that God, who hath so often said to my soul, *Quare morieris?* Why wilt thou die? and so often sworn to my soul, *Vivit Dominus*, As the Lord liveth, I would not have thee die, but live, will neither let me die, nor let me live, but die an everlasting life, and live an everlasting death; that that God, who, when he could not get into me, by standing, and knocking, by his ordinary means of entering, by his word, his mercies, hath applied his judgements, and hath shaked the house, this body, with agues and palsies, and set this house on fire, with fevers and calentures, and frighted the master of the house, my soul, with horrors, and heavy apprehensions, and so made an entrance into me; That that God should lose and frustrate all his own purposes and practices upon me, and leave me, and cast me away, as though I had cost him nothing, that this God at last, should let this soul go away, as a smoke, as a vapour, as a bubble, and that then this soul cannot be a smoke, nor a vapour, nor a bubble, but must lie in darkness, as long as the Lord of light is light itself, and never a spark of that light reach to my soul; What Tophet is not Paradise, what brimstone is not amber, what gnashing is not a comfort, what gnawing of the worm is not a tickling, what torment is not a marriage bed to this damnation, to be secluded eternally, eternally, eternally from the sight of God?

Easter Day 1622

I scarce know a place of Scripture, more diversly read, and consequently more variously interpreted than that place, which should most enlighten us, in this consideration presently under our hands; which is that place to the Corinthians, *Non omnes dormiemus, We shall not all sleep, but we shall all be changed.* The apostle professes there to deliver us a mystery, (*Behold, I show you a mystery*) but translators and expositors have multiplied mystical clouds upon the words. St Chrysostom reads these words as we do, *Non dormiemus, We shall not all sleep*, but thereupon he argues, and concludes, that we shall not all die. The common reading of the ancients is contrary to that, *Omnes dormiemus, sed non, &c. We shall all sleep, but we shall not all be changed.* The vulgate edition in the Roman Church differs from both, and as much from the original, as from either, *Omnes resurgemus, We shall all rise again, but we shall not all be changed.* St Jerome examines the two readings, and then leaves the reader to his choice, as a thing indifferent. St Augustine doth so too, and concludes *æquè Catholicos esse*, That they are as good Catholics that read it the one way, as the other. But howsoever, that which St Chrysostom collects upon his reading, may not be maintained. He reads as we do; and without all doubt aright, *We shall not all sleep*; But what then? Therefore

245

shall we not all die? To sleep there, is to rest in the grave, to continue in the state of the dead, and so we shall not all sleep, not continue in the state of the dead. But yet, *Statutum est*, says the apostle, as verily as Christ was once offered to bear our sins, so verily *is it appointed to every man once to die*; And, as verily *as by one man, sin entered into the world, and death by sin*, so verily *death passed upon all men, for that all men have sinned*; So the apostle institutes the comparison, so he constitutes the doctrine, in those two places of Scripture, As verily as Christ died for all, all shall die, As verily as every man sins, every man shall die.

In that change then, which we who are then alive, shall receive, (for though we shall not all sleep, we shall all be changed) we shall have a present dissolution of body and soul, and that is truly a death, and a present redintegration of the same body and the same soul, and that is truly a resurrection; we shall die, and be alive again, before another could consider that we were dead; but yet this shall not be done in an absolute instant; some succession of time, though undiscernible there is. It shall be done *In raptu*, in a rapture; but even in a rapture there is a motion, a transition from one to another place. It shall be done, says he, *In ictu oculi*, *In the twinkling of an eye*; But even in the twinkling of an eye, there is a shutting of the eye-lids, and an opening of them again; Neither of these is done in an absolute instant, but requires some succession of time. The apostle, in the resurrection in our text, constitutes a *Prius*, something to be done first, and something after; first those that were dead in Christ shall rise first, and then, Then when that is done, after that, not all at once, we that are alive shall be wrought upon, we shall be changed, our change comes after their rising; so in our change there is a *Prius* too, first we shall be dissolved, (so we die) and then we shall be re-compact, (so we rise again). This is the difference, they that sleep in the grave, put off, and depart with the very substance of the body, it is no longer flesh, but dust, they that are changed at the last day, put off, and depart with, only the qualities of the body, as mortality and corruption; It is still the same body, without resolving into dust, but the first step that it makes, is into glory . . .

Lincoln's Inn, Easter Term 1620

After that curse upon the serpent, *super pectus gradieris*, upon thy belly shalt thou go, we shall as soon see a serpent go upright, and not crawl, as, after that judgment, *In pulverem reverteris*, to dust thou shalt return, see a man, that shall not see death, and corruption in death. Corruption upon our skin, says the text, (our outward beauty;) corruption upon our body, (our whole strength, and constitution.) And, this cor-

247

ruption, not a green paleness, not a yellow jaundice, not a blue lividness, not a black morphew upon our skin, not a bony leanness, not a sweaty faintness, not an ungracious decrepitness upon our body, but a destruction, a destruction to both, *After my skin my body shall be destroyed.* Though not destroyed by being resolved to ashes in the fire, (perchance I shall not be burnt) not destroyed by being washed to slime, in the sea, (perchance I shall not be drowned) but destroyed contemptibly, by those whom I breed, and feed, by worms; (*After my skin worms shall destroy my body.*) And thus far our case is equal; one event to the good and bad; worms shall destroy all in them all. And farther than this, their case is equal too, for, they shall both rise again from this destruction. But in this lies the future glory, in this lies the present comfort of the saints of God, that, *after all this,* (so that this is not my last act, to die, nor my last scene, to lie in the grave, nor my last *exit,* to go out of the grave) *after,* says Job; And indefinitely, *After,* I know not how soon, nor how late, I press not into God's secrets for that; but, *after, all this, Ego,* I, I that speak now, and shall not speak then, silenced in the grave, I that see now, and shall not see then, *ego videbo,* I shall see, (I shall have a new faculty) *videbo Deum,* I shall see God (I shall have a new object) and, *In carne,* I shall see him in the flesh, (I shall have a new organ, and a new medium) and, *In carne mea,* that flesh shall be *my flesh,* (I shall have a new propriety in that flesh) this flesh which I have now, is not mine, but the worms; but that flesh shall be so mine, as I shall never divest it more, but *In my flesh, I shall see God for ever . . .*

If thou hadst seen the bodies of men rise out of the grave, at Christ's resurrection, could that be a stranger thing to thee, than, (if thou hadst never seen, nor heard, nor imagined it before) to see an oak that spreads so far, rise out of an acorn? Or if churchyards did vent themselves every spring, and that there were such a resurrection of bodies every year, when thou hadst seen as many resurrections as years, the resurrection would be no stranger to thee, than the spring is . . .

If the whole body were an eye, or an ear, where were the body, says Saint Paul; but, when of the whole body there is neither eye nor ear, nor any member left, where is the body? And what should an eye do there, where there is nothing to be seen but loathsomness; or a nose there, where there is nothing to be smelt, but putrefaction; or an ear, where in the grave they do not praise God? Doth not that body that boasted but yesterday of that privilege above all creatures, that it only could go upright, lie today as flat upon the earth as the body of a horse, or of a dog? And doth it not tomorrow lose his other privilege, of looking up to heaven? Is it not farther removed from the eye of heaven, The sun, than any dog, or horse, by being covered with the earth, which they are not? Painters have presented to us with some horror, the skeleton, the frame of the bones of a man's body; but the state of a body, in the dissolution of the grave, no pencil can present to us. Between that excremental jelly that thy body is made of at first, and that jelly which thy body dissolves to at last; there is not so noisome, so putrid a thing in nature . . .

Thy skin, and thy body shall be ground away, trod away upon the ground. Ask where the iron is that is ground off of a knife, or axe; Ask that marble that is worn off of the threshold in the church-porch by continual treading, and with that iron, and with that marble, thou mayest find thy father's skin and body; *Contrita sunt*, The knife, the marble, the skin, the body are ground away, trod away, they are destroyed, who knows the revolutions of dust? Dust upon the King's highway, and dust upon the King's grave, are both, or neither, Dust Royal, and may change places; who knows the revolutions of dust? . . .

We pass on. As in *Massa damnata*, the whole lump of mankind is under the condemnation of Adam's sin, and yet the good purpose of God severs some men from that condemnation, so, at the resurrection, all shall rise; but not all to glory. But, amongst them, that do *Ego*, says Job, I shall. I, as I am the same man, made up of the same body, and the same soul. Shall I imagine a difficulty in my body, because I have lost an arm in the East, and a leg in the West? because I have left some blood in the North, and some bones in the South? Do but remember, with what ease you have sat in the chair, casting an account, and made a shilling on one hand, a pound on the other, or five shillings below, ten above, because all these lay easily within your reach. Consider how much less, all this earth is to him, that sits in heaven, and spans all this world, and reunites in an instant arms, and legs, blood, and bones, in what corners so ever they be scattered. The greater work may seem to be in reducing the soul; That that soul which sped so ill in that body, last time it came to it, as that it contracted original sin then, and was put to the slavery to serve that body, and to serve it in the ways of sin, not for an apprenticeship of seven, but seventy years after, that that soul after it hath once got loose by death, and lived God knows how many thousands of years, free from that body, that abused it so before, and in the sight and fruition of that God, where it was in no danger, should willingly, nay desirously, ambitiously seek this scattered body, this Eastern, and Western, and Northern, and Southern body, this is the most inconsiderable consideration; and yet, *Ego*, I, I the same body, and the same soul, shall be recompact again, and be identically, numerically, individually the same man. The same integrity of body, and soul, and the same integrity in the organs of my body, and in the faculties of my soul too; I shall be all there, my body, and my soul, and all my body, and all my soul. I am not all here, I am here now preaching upon this text, and I am at home in my library considering whether St Gregory, or St Jerome, have said best of this text, before. I am here speaking to you, and yet I consider by the way, in the same instant, what it is likely you will say to one another, when I have done. You are not all here neither; you are here now, hearing me, and yet you are thinking that you have heard a better sermon somewhere else, of this text before; you are here, and yet you think you could have heard some other doctrine of downright predestination, and reprobation roundly delivered somewhere else with more edification to you; you are here, and you remember your selves that now ye think of it, this had been the fittest time, now, when everybody else is at church, to have made such and such a private visit; and because you would be there, you are there. I cannot say, you cannot say so perfectly, so entirely now, as at the Resurrection, *Ego*, I am here; I, body and soul; I, soul and faculties; as Christ said to *Peter, Noli timere, Ego sum, Fear nothing, it is I*; so I say to myself, *Noli timere*; My soul, why art thou so sad, my body, why dost thou languish? *Ego*, I, body and soul, soul and faculties, shall say to Christ Jesus, *Ego sum*, Lord, it is I, and he shall not say, *Nescio te, I know thee not*, but avow me, and place me at his right hand. *Ego sum, I am the man that hath seen affliction, by the rod of his wrath*;

Ego sum, and I the same man, shall receive the crown of glory which shall not fade . . .

It shall be *Caro mea*, my flesh, so, as that nothing can draw it from the allegiance of my God; and *Caro mea*, *My flesh*, so, as that nothing can divest me of it. Here a bullet will ask a man, where's your arm; and a wolf will ask a woman, where's your breast? A sentence in the Star Chamber will ask him, where's your ear, and a month's close prison will ask him, where's your flesh? a fever will ask him, where's your red, and a morphew will ask him, where's your white? But when after all this, when *after my skin worms shall destroy my body, I shall see God*, I shall see him in my flesh, which shall be mine as inseparably, (in the effect, though not in the manner) as the hypostatical union of God, and man, in Christ, makes our nature and the Godhead one person in him. My flesh shall no more be none of mine, than Christ shall not be man, as well as God.

INDEX OF FIRST LINES